Mandalas of the World

A MEDITATING & PAINTING GUIDE

Rudiger Dahlke

D0128151

Drawings by
Rudiger Dahlke & Katharina von Martius

Sterling Publishing Co., Inc.   New York

ACKNOWLEDGMENTS

For the foreword and the many ideas I thank Thorwald. To Carmen and Math I owe my thanks for our long road together, on which years ago was born the idea for the Mandala-Book; to Kerstin for suggestions, criticism, and ideas, and the capability to express (p. 142) the Whole in few words. To Oskar I owe the right suggestions at the right moment; Niki and the Roberts I thank for examination and criticism; my mother for suggestions and the many retypings. I am grateful to Katharina not only that she was always there, but also for her great patience, for the many photographs, and for her drawings.

Translated by Annette Englander
Edited by Cornelia M. Parkinson

Library of Congress Cataloging-in-Publication Data

Dahlke, Rüdiger.
   [Mandalas der Welt. English]
   Mandalas of the world : a meditating and painting guide / Rudiger Dahlke ; drawings by Rudiger Dahlke & Katharina von Martius.
      p.   cm.
   Translation of: Mandalas der Welt.
   Includes index.
   ISBN 0-8069-8526-7 (hard)
   1. Mandalas. 2. Meditation. 3. Art and religion. 4. Spiritual life. I. Title.
BL604.M36D34   1992
291.3'7—dc20   91-42009
                                        CIP

English translation © 1992 by Sterling Publishing Company
387 Park Avenue South, New York, N.Y. 10016
Original edition published in German under the title
Mandalas der Welt: Ein Meditations- und Malbuch
© 1985 by Heinrich Hugendubel Verlag, München
Distributed in Canada by Sterling Publishing
% Canadian Manda Group, P.O. Box 920, Station U
Toronto, Ontario, Canada M8Z 5P9
Distributed in Great Britain and Europe by Cassell PLC
Villiers House, 41/47 Strand, London WC2N 5JE
Distributed in Australia by Capricorn Link Ltd.
P.O. Box 704, Windsor, NSW 2756, Australia
Printed in U.S.A.
All rights reserved

Sterling ISBN 0-8069-8526-7

CONTENTS

FOREWORD

The true center of a circle is a point. A point has neither dimension nor place. Thus, the point withdraws from our perception as well as from our imagination. It does not belong to our world—because in our world everything has extension and dimension, because our world is form.

The point belongs to another order of being. It exists beyond our world. It is metaphysical in the literal sense. The point symbolizes unity, independent existence, perfection—it is therefore in almost all cultures and times also a symbol for God.

The point contains everything, but only in the potential, not in the manifest condition. Circle and globe are born from it; they are forms of revelation of the point. What is still metaphysical potential in the point comes, through circle and globe, into form.

The circle is a point plus dimension; therefore the circle lives through its central point, and is defined by it—even when we cannot comprehend this point. The point and the circle—God and the world—the one and the many—the unmanifest and the manifest—content and form—the metaphysical and the physical—all these terms mean the same.

One need only think of the relation of the seed to the grown plant in order to realize that the whole is already contained in the part. We human beings always need dimensions—the world of visible forms—in order to recognize therein the invisible. Thus we need a body in order to be able to experience our consciousness. The world of the visible is the vehicle that lets us come into contact with transcendence.

God manifests Himself in the world, the Christians would say; and in Buddhist thought Nirvana and Prakriti are identical. Sufi master Ibn Arabi means the same thing when he says: "With certainty nothing else exists but God the Almighty, his qualities and his actions. Everything belongs to him, stems from him, and moves towards him. Were he separated from the world for the period of the twinkle of an eye, the world would disappear at this moment. The world can exist only through the fact that he preserves it and watches over it. Indeed, he creates the light, so powerful that it exceeds our capability of perception; and we can only recognize his creation, which disguises him." (Ibn Arabi, *Journey to the Master of Power.*)

Comprehension of this paradoxical connection between reality and illusion can save us from extreme behavior, to which we too willingly submit. Either we lose ourselves in the world of form (materialism) or we try to flee from the world of form into the illusion that one could find "outside of the world"—spirituality. But we cannot flee from the world, since it only exists in our minds. Therefore, we have to use the world for our path to the center, to salvation. To use the world means to live in it, to consciously come to terms with it—to work in it, to play with it, to dance with it—and thus take it as a pathway to find the point in which the diversity unites.

The law of the world is movement, the law of the center is peace. Life in the world is movement, activity, dance. Our life is a constant dance around the center, a constant circling around the Invisible One, to which we—just like the circle—owe our existence. We live out of the center-point—even when we cannot perceive it—and we long for it. The circle cannot forget its origin. We also long for Paradise. Whatever we do, we do it because we seek our center—the Center.

Behind every act is the wish for change—a dissatisfaction with our lot. As long as human beings are in the world, they will always act, always change, because in the world there cannot be any constant satisfaction. Only by reaching the center, by entering the point, are we redeemed and freed of our dissatisfaction.

But where can one find this point? Nowhere, since it has no place. Everywhere, since it is the basis of all being. We have to learn to draw our circles, to let them get tighter and tighter, until our whole life circles around the point. It's no accident that the Old Greek word for "to sin" also means "to miss the point." If we miss the center, we live in sin, because we are separated from God.

It is necessary to overcome this separation, to bridge over this abyss. The steady circling around the invisible center is the archetypical pattern of our life, and it is the basic pattern of the dance. The dance is a ritual, an imitation of human life. Thus, one can use the dance (as the dervishes do, for example) as a means to achieve mystical experiences. But other rites—such as the serpentine procession or the priest's circling of the altar—have the same underlying symbolic meaning: *the dance around the center.*

This book also deals with a rite. It is not primarily a book to read, but a book that invites you to ritually circle around the center. It is therefore an unusual book—a book that wants more than just to be read and understood. It wants to lead to experiences. It wants to expand the consciousness. We can do justice to the term "Painting-Book" only if we understand painting as a rite, as the microcosmic imitation of a forever valid original pattern. Every act remains meaningless and senseless until we comprehend it as a rite.

Only when we become aware that every human action is a formal expression of content and the pattern behind it, do we begin to comprehend our life as rite. Then suddenly we realize that it is not so important **what** we do, but **how** we do it. Zen monks make such "simple" acts as sitting, walking, drinking tea and shooting arrows into rituals, and thus transform their acts into teaching devices on their path.

The intention of this book is to teach you, not how to paint pictures with nice colors, but how to perform this act so consciously that one discovers the Whole in the part.

Rudiger Dahlke has looked at the most diverse forms, and has suddenly seen in everything the original pattern of the Being—the Mandala. He now invites you in this book to consciously interact with this pattern. We all constantly dance around the center—but we have to bring more and more of our awareness into experiencing the laws of the dance. This book could very well help in doing that.

Enough said, it is time for movement.

Thorwald Dethlefsen
Munich

PREFACE

This book that you just opened is not even a finished book yet! In contrast to most other books, it still needs your collaboration and willingness to find its true form. Yes, this time instead of reading a book, you actually entered on a path.

Neither will you find a structure at the beginning—that structure or order will become evident on your path. This path also does not lead straight from the beginning to the end, but rotates in circles and spirals around the center—that center that is also your own. The path of this book will come close to the center and then withdraw from it—it will touch and then let go again—it will travel around in a circle—according to the Mandala. If you go around with it and follow its spiral windings, you will not feel dizzy. But whenever you offer resistance to the "dance around the center," you will experience this resistance as discomfort—you will feel dizzy—maybe even lose your way.

The outer path results from theory and practice and, here especially, from painting and meditation exercises. Whenever there is something to paint, you will come across the following sign: ▭◦ References to these and other exercises are also marked with a line on the left side, such as you find next to this paragraph. If you follow these outer guideposts trustfully, everything else will resolve by itself.

PRE-HISTORY

It is not our intention to lay out before you everything we know about Mandalas. Wherever information comes up, it is meant to be a suggestion—or a stimulus—that may take you deeper in one or the other direction. We will only touch upon some major areas of knowledge and leave out others entirely. Some we will merely observe from a distance. So, as you can see, it is not important for you to absorb all suggestions—not even to understand all of them. The goal of this path is not the understanding, but the *experience* of the Mandala.

This book wants to become the Ariadne-thread to guide you through your personal labyrinth: a guide to your own Mandalas, to the experience of the universe as Mandala.

As long as necessary, this path will be accompanied by my words, but much more important is your willingness to open up to your own experiences, to find your own way and to play the game.

In fact this book should become a toy for you. If you are of the opinion that you are too old to play—too far beyond the time for coloring books—ask yourself if you are also too old for "the path" and "the life." Playing is not so easy—most adults have long unlearned it, and to do it now intentionally is exhausting because, like the meditation, the play also lives through unintention.

Meditation and play have several things in common. Meditation deals with the center. Most games circle around a center. Children play out of their inner center—and out of it they bring almost unlimited energy and joy. Games such as "Ring Around the Rosie," jump rope, the Hula Hoop or spinning the top illustrate this principle. All these games are of course behind us; but if we take a closer look, we see that adults also enjoy dancing around the center—except that they make it tougher on themselves.

Take a look at the "rides" at a country fair, for example. Many of these complicated vehicles trace their origins back to the carousel, which revolves around a center. And, if you feel too grown-up for that, you might like to try hitting the bull's-eye at a shooting gallery, or getting together with some friends in a cozy mood at a round table. In many dances, the moment of the turn around one's own center plays the decisive role—most distinctly in the waltz. And the waltz has maintained its outstanding popularity through the years—because children and adults both enjoy dancing around their own center.

But all these situations depict Mandalas in movement.

To reset the inner Mandala into movement is one of my objects—but, as the author of this book, I cannot really do for my readers anything that they are not willing to do for themselves. This book of Mandalas makes that especially clear—because at first it might appear boring and colorless. It will remain this way if you will not let your energy flow into it and make it **your** book. But then it can reflect your total inner diversity and colorfulness and can become your most individual and your very own book—possibly the first one that you yourself ever created.

✦ THE CHOICE ✦

When you experience resistance to the "unfamiliar" structures presented in this book, make yourself aware of what you are doing right from the beginning. This is the basic situation that we find ourselves up against—we face again and again seemingly unfamiliar structures which we perceive as rules, instructions, restraints, and laws "on the outside." One possibility is to fight against these structures, but there is another choice. We can also accept them and make them our own—yes, *recognize* them as our own—and finally experience that everything is always "only" imitation—imitation of what already was and is and will be.

This path demands victims. Already now we are challenged to sacrifice our illusion, so that it is possible to create something of our own—something new—out of our freedom. This realization may be depressing at the beginning but, experienced in its total depth, it is "only" liberating.

A guru expressed this in the following parable:

The family of the white clouds that float in the blue sky divides itself into two groups: on the one side is the large group of clouds whose goal is to get to the warm South. They suffer a lot, especially when the wind blows them north, west, or east. On the other side there is a small group that has realized that it is their destination as clouds to be driven by the wind. They have no goal, *or only one:* to follow their path, their destination, the wind—and thus they are always in harmony with themselves and the goal.

But at the end of the day all the clouds are at the same place.

✦ THE PARADOX ✦

Here, now, decide for yourself: do you have a reading and textbook in front of you? Or an experience-and-"to-do" book? In case you chose the first version (maybe thinking: "I will read that now; my wife can fill in the colors; she has more time), it is probably best that you stop reading immediately after this paragraph and leave it to that someone else who has the time. Because what I really have in mind—"the path back to the center"—is an idea; and my courage to do this book grows out of the hope that this idea can be read between the lines, that it speaks out of the pictures, and comes across in the exercises.

I trust that those who want to accompany me on this path already carry this idea in themselves, and that step by step they will remember, as the idea in me meets the idea in you and unites with it. The One, the center of the Mandala, withdraws itself from all intellectual presentations, but nevertheless lives in all of us. We will not be able to find it with the help of our willpower or our intellect, but those two faculties take part in the process: they get a sense and a task. Unfortunately, willpower and intellect do not suffice. Also, our language, which usually expresses our thinking fairly well, does not facilitate the path to the center. On the contrary, it seems that it leads us away further and further, that it engages us more and more in the "world of the ten thousand things." Even so, our language is helping us, because the further it leads us away, the closer it also leads us. That sounds like a paradox; it is one.

Let's put ourselves into the following situation: We take a jet plane and remove ourselves from a point of the Mandala earth, going more and more in one direction. The farther we travel from that starting point, the closer we are moving back to it—in the world we live in—the world of the Mandalas.

◆ THE SYMBOL ◆

It is all right for us to entrust ourselves to language, since we know that it leads us indirectly, because language lives through images. But pictures and symbols can lead us directly. Circle, wheel and Mandala are, after all, symbols. The intellect may go with us on this journey, and it may have fun, especially since it will have to remain uncomprehending when confronted by the Essential.

The symbol always contains everything: i.e., both sides of the polarity. Thus, for example, **Ra** stands for radium itself, without distinguishing between its life-supporting and life-destroying qualities. In other words, the symbol does not exclude, but it includes; it does not restrict as words and numbers do. This way it can never satisfy the intellect, since that thrives on exclusion and distinction.

The symbol contains the paradox in itself and is therefore truer than everything else in the world of Maya, the world of appearances.

We want to get closer to the symbol consciously. The key to that is so close that it already may see banal to us. We may not even want to bother with such simple things, but nevertheless everything *is* simple.

It is this center we will deal with. We will travel far, through various cultures and times, but still we will be concerned only with this one center. It will meet us at the most diverse places and in the most unexpected guises, but still it will always be the one center.

There will be no danger in getting lost for a while in foreign parts. Let's remember the parable of the lost son: All paths lead back again, and so we will also experience that all journeys, exercises, and experiences always lead back to the One.

When God had completed the Creation out of the One, in his hand he finally held the key to all that was created. It was now the task of the human being to find this key.

In order to enhance the mystery, he wanted to hide it as well as possible. He asked the heavenly advisors for ideas, and they suggested plenty of places—as far away as the moon.

But God spoke:

"I want to hide it very close by and still very far away, where they will look for it last." And he hid it in the center of the human being.

THE WORLD OF MANDALAS
MANDALAS OF THE WORLD

To rediscover as your own the forms and symbols that we came across on this journey will be easier and easier in time, because these structures are universal. They don't belong to anybody and they jointly belong to everybody. They are the basic elements of creation, part of everything and at the same time also the Whole. After all, the universe itself is a Mandala consisting of countless Mandalas of the most varying dimensions. Here is a spiral nebula.

13

Each Mandala is at the same time Universe. As the word says:

the one and the diverse.

Or:

Out of the one grows the diversity. Behind all diversity lies the One.

Also our own tighter universe, our solar system, is a Mandala.

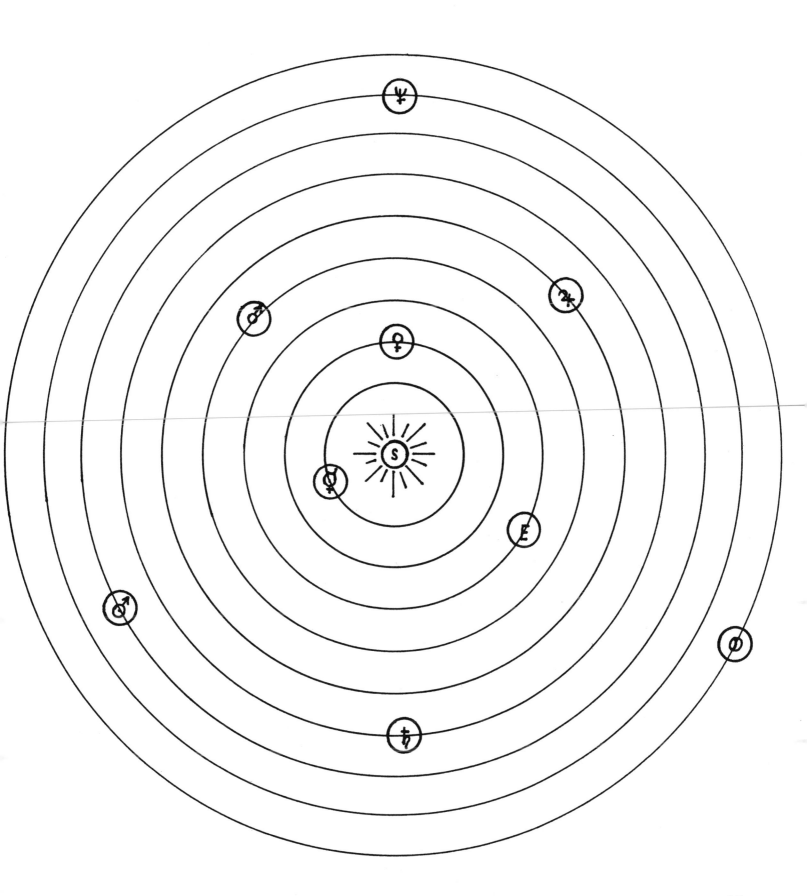

As we can see already, our earth is a Mandala. If we come closer, we find the oceans of the world. Their elements are water-drops—and thus Mandalas. The firm structures, the land and the mountains, are built from minerals. Their basic elements are the crystals—and many crystals again form Mandalas.

Here is such a crystal-Mandala.

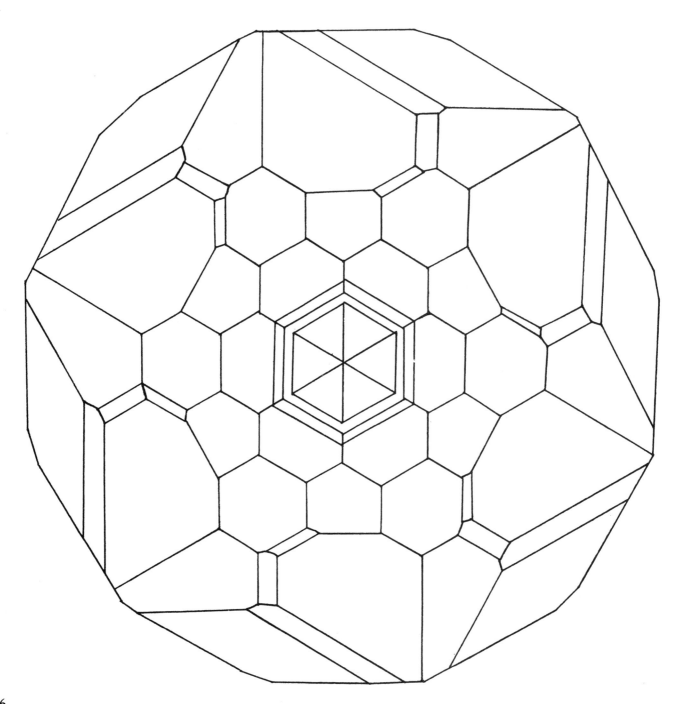

Everything alive—plants, animals, and human beings—
consists of cells. Each cell is a Mandala.

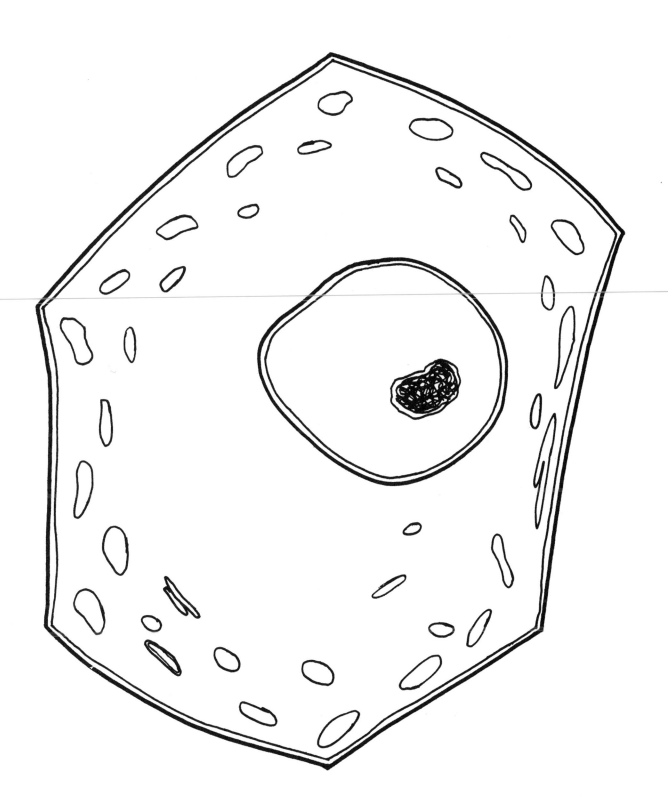

Every cell has a nucleus, and this one is a Mandala. The division of this nucleus leads to two new cell-Mandalas. This way grows the living world of the Mandalas.

Here is a cell-nucleus in the process of cell division.

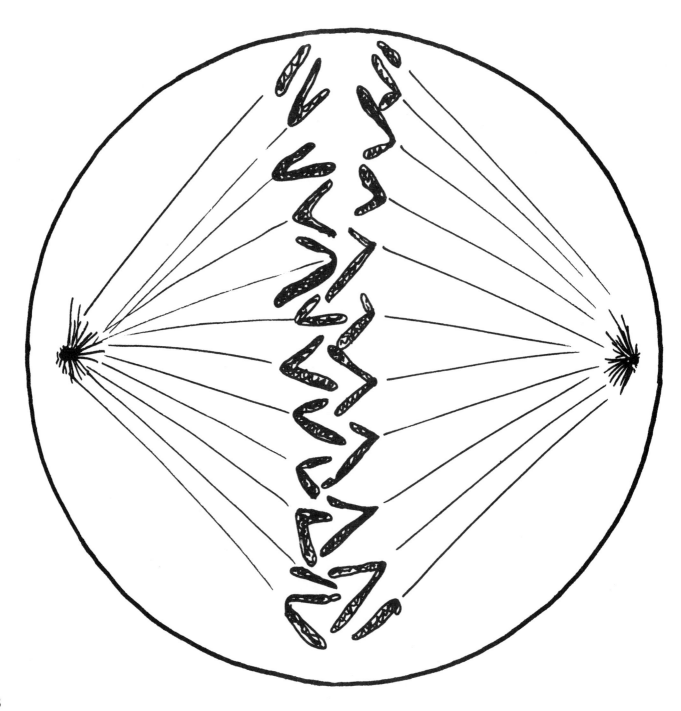

All cells and crystals and everything on this planet consist of atoms, and each atom is a Mandala.

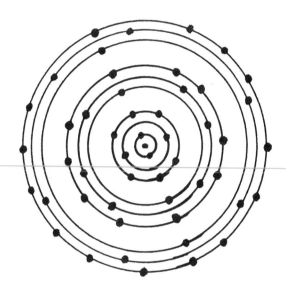

After the atom, the scale becomes too small for us, and we do not recognize the next-smaller structures. A similar thing happens when the structures become too big.

Not too long ago, the structure of the Mandala of the atoms—and even longer ago, also the one of the cell and the spiral nebula—was unknown to us. But does it mean that because we didn't know of it, it did not exist? It certainly did exist. We see it in the rose windows of Gothic architecture and even earlier. We see it in the Celtic motif on the facing page.

• THE RED THREAD—AS ON THE OUTSIDE, SO ON THE INSIDE •

No matter how far our modern researches advance, they find "only" the same basic patterns that we already can find in ourselves. As above so below—as on the outside so on the inside. We cannot avoid this timeless law as we explore the Mandala; and it will be, above all, our own experience that we will be concerned with. Our subject makes that easy. In fact, it is actually difficult to become absorbed in a Mandala and remain unaffected by it. It is equally difficult to look at a rose window of a Gothic cathedral without being touched by it.

Yes, it is almost impossible to create Mandalas without being moved inwardly. The Mandala *is* movement—is a wheel of life—the image of the universe, constantly emerging from the one center, striving towards the outside and at the same time converging out of the diversity to the one center. Every person recognizes this basic pattern, because it is carried within the Self.

It is easy to open up to this understanding, and we want to keep to an easy path. If you make this book to your own—if you want to search for your path—then from now on, you have "only" to make sure that form and content stay in harmony. Take the tasks that come towards you, really just as they come: without judging them. ("This is too childish for me." It cannot become "childlike" and playful enough.)

It's worthwhile to work right through. Don't try to smuggle yourself past it, or leave out or skip Mandalas. Instead, go step by step consciously painting, reading, creating, through the labyrinth of the book, which by itself is a Mandala—and thus you spin a magic red thread through your own inner maze.

Now paint your path into this French garden-labyrinth. And experience, while doing this, the meaning of abbreviations, improvements, paths and detours.

Paint the fantasy-Mandala on the opposite page from the inside to the outside. Follow your spontaneous inspirations and ideas concerning color and material. The structure itself may serve as a pointer or guidepost. Even if it seems to you imperfect and defective, accept it for the time being and experience what comes of it. Just as the pattern may be technically imperfect, your execution may have technical deficiencies. Allow that—after all, technique is not what this is all about. The patterns intentionally have not been created by specialists. It is meaningless to leave the execution to experts—this book is about yourself.

◆ QUESTIONS ◆

Think back to the painting of your (perhaps) first Mandala and how you experienced yourself while doing it.

Look at yourself. Do you stay within the given structures and limits? Or do you tend to surpass them, or revolt against the pattern?

Do you allow yourself to make "mistakes"?

Or do you get angry at yourself when you make them?

Or do you look for somebody to turn against in your dissatisfaction?

Do you like to start in the center or from the outside? Or somewhere else?

Do you take your time? Or do you hurry?

Which colors did you use?

Do you like your work? Or are you dissatisfied with it?

Do you recognize yourself in it? Would you enjoy recognizing yourself in your own picture?

Do you feel like going on? Or was it already too much?

Do you try to be totally conscious with yourself? And especially honest?

After all, who besides yourself can you fool?

◆ ANSWERS ◆

As you might be anticipating already, the Mandala can answer countless questions, questions about you and God and the world. You can read everything in it, once you have developed the viewpoint for it. If you read, it does not matter at all what interests you: the horoscope, the coffee grounds, the *I Ching*, the hereditary substance (DNA), or a Mandala. You only have to be able to do it. You will not be able to do it satisfactorily after this first Mandala, but the more intensively you occupy yourself with Mandalas, the more your ability to see and to define will grow. You will not at all be able to stop this process. And this activity, in which intellect and intuition each play a part, is neither good nor bad—after all, this is not what it is all about!

It would be fun, of course, to see more than others, to look more successfully. But we shall be concerned with the *real* view into the Essential, with the path. That, at the beginning, may seem less fun, may even appear to be difficult and burdensome. When we occupy ourselves with the Mandala, we deal with a **perfect** form. If we really devote ourselves to this process, it will greatly affect our own perfection, even if the procedure is at first only an external one.

We find something similar in the body exercises of the Hatha Yoga. They probably resulted from the fact that the bodies of developed people spontaneously took on these attitudes because they corresponded with the perfect inner attitude. Today's reverse path is not wrong: one takes on a perfect external attitude (Asana) hoping that the corresponding inner attitude will grow in the same way. In fact, the perfection of the Lotus posture alone helps to create for everyone a harmonization of body and soul.

Therefore, when we occupy ourselves with a Mandala, its perfect structure has similar effects on our own structure.

◆ THE HUMAN BEING AND THE CENTERS ◆

The human body is built of cells, and those, in turn, are built of atoms. That means that our bodies are actually made up of innumerable atoms. But we can also understand our body as Mandala. With outstretched arms and legs we form a five-pointed star; and each star is a Mandala. As a star-Mandala, each person has a clearly recognizable center; and we are all constantly in search of it. Sometimes we find it. The center—whether we feel it consciously or not—recognizes that Mandala-structure as something identical to its own nature.

We perceive the conscious experience of our center as indescribable happiness: it is the goal of each meditation. After all, each meditation is a circling around the center and therefore a Mandala. And each Mandala is a recollection of its own center and thus a meditation.

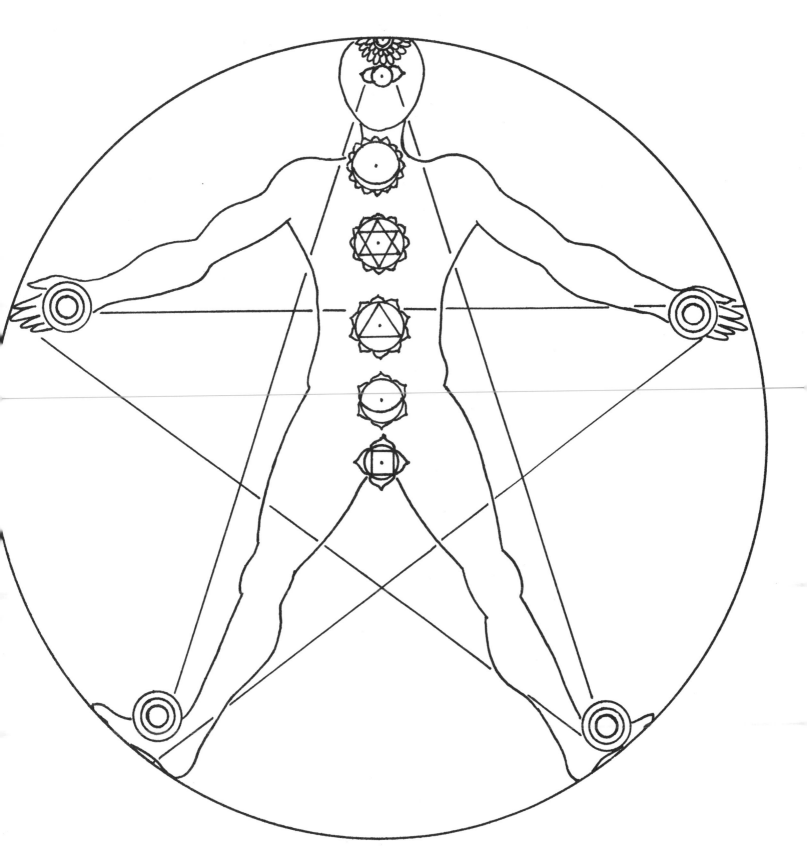

ORIGIN OF THE MANDALA

To say something about the history of the Mandala is difficult, because history deals with time—and the Mandala exists, as its shape will teach us, essentially beyond time and space. The history of the Mandala would have to begin, just like every proper history, with its origin. But that is unknown. The Mandala cannot be fitted into time. Yes, it may be observed in time, but it always has the tendency to pull us into its center, where time and space come to an end.

Of course, we can try to determine the occurrence of Mandalas in time. A very early Mandala might have been the impact of some meteor plunging into a primitive ocean.

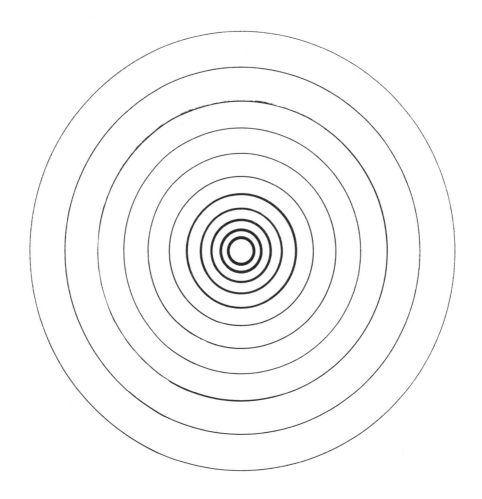

We must admit that the Mandala is older than we are. Yes, it is as old as our world—as old as the Creation. Don't the scientists tell us that everything started with a big bang? And isn't the picture of an explosion also a Mandala?

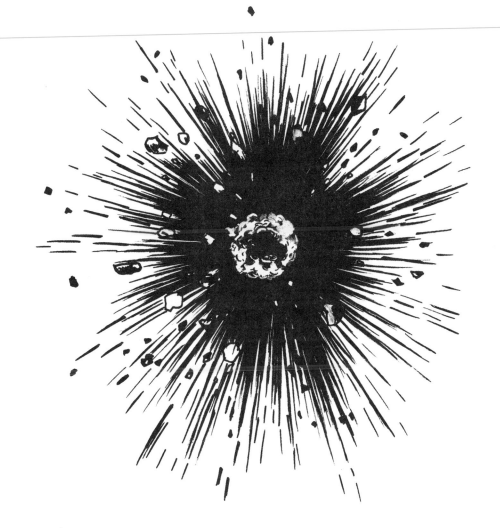

In fact, scientists have verified that our universe has expanded more and more after the original explosion. It may be even more astonishing that for millennia this knowledge has been handed down through Hindu tradition. The Creation is described as the breathing rhythm of Brahma: he inhales and exhales it, he lets it come into existence and disappear in a constant succession.

Looking at the cyclical nature of this tradition, we can assume that the seers and *rishis* who composed the Vedas, the foundation of the Hindu religions, saw even further than our modern science, because everything in creation develops in cycles.

Looking at other myths of creation, we find the same themes, only in other words—which should not particularly astonish us, since despite the many languages, there is only **one** truth.

In the Gospel of St. John it is written: "In the beginning was the Word." In the Indian language it was a sound. Also, behind the Word, a sound is hidden, and behind this a Mandala, because from the one center the sound waves travel spherically, and the same picture is being created as when a stone is thrown into the water—but this time it is in space.

In other myths everything begins with the light. Now every spark, every light is also a Mandala, its vibrations radiating in all directions from the one center.

We also find the history of the Creation depicted graphically and symbolically in many of the Gothic window rosettes. The architects of the Gothic period intentionally used the Mandala, because hardly any other symbol is better suited for portraying the cyclical character of the Creation and the connection of transcendence (in the centerpoint) and polarity (in the periphery of the rose).

A good example is the rose of the Cathedral of Lausanne. The next drawing shows the stony structure that is partially expressed in the lead-frames of the windows.

Pay attention, when painting, how all forms of this Mandala come into existence out of the center and how they maintain their relationship to this imaginary center.

No matter how we twist and turn the creation, we do not find anything *before* the Mandala. Rather, through the Mandala, we do find something before the original explosion, since this explosion, with its never-ending "WHY," doesn't provide satisfactory answers to the scientific question "Why was there suddenly an explosion?" The researchers remain occupied with their scientific Zen Koan: What existed first, the hen or the egg? As there is no logical solution for the Zen Koan, so there is none for the scientific Koan. The solution lies rather in the center of the Mandala and is only accessible to the experience.

Now try to draw the center-points into the following circles and soap bubbles:

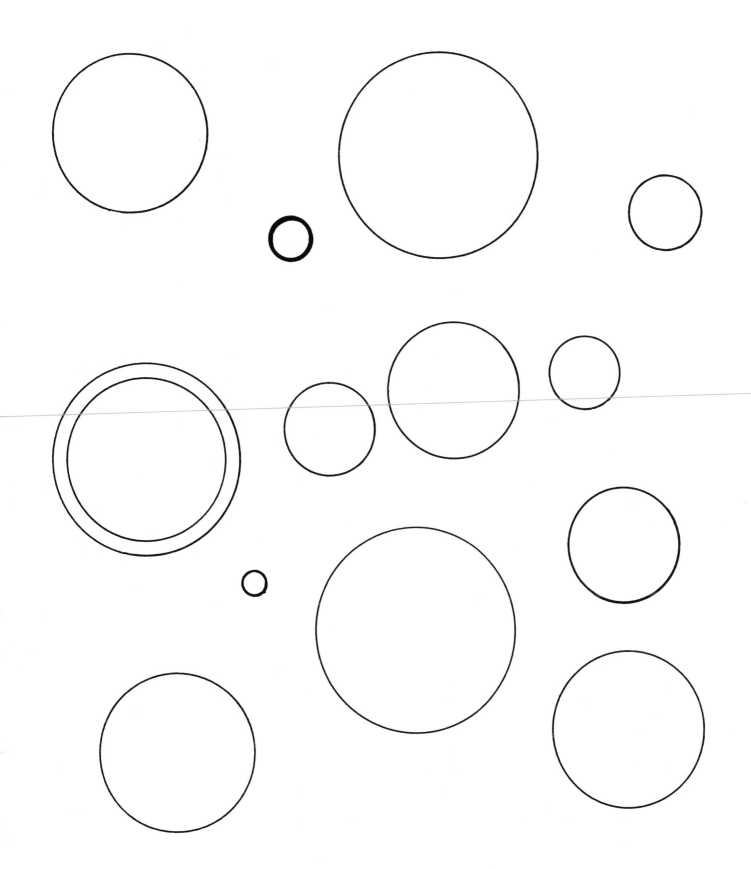

◆ THE POINT OF ORIGIN ◆

It is not only difficult to determine a center-point, it is impossible to depict a real point. Because although all forms derive from the point, the point itself has no form. According to definition, the point has no dimension relating to space (is not three-dimensional); it belongs to the realm of the ideas, not to the realm of form.

We cannot perceive the point at all—just as we cannot see the pure, white light. What we generally call point already goes beyond the idea. The little piece of graphite in the pencil, with which we draw the point, already has dimension relating to space and thus is not a point anymore, but already rather a circle or even a globe. In this way a globe develops from the point, as soon as we provide it with space. If we also include time, we then have our creation, the world of Maya illusion. If we take space and time (the two deceivers, as the Indians call them) out of it again, then the whole world of illusion will give way and sink into the one original point. Again we realize that the creation is "only" a Mandala.

If we continue to develop the point horizontally or vertically, we get a straight line, a distance. If we continue this straight line forever, finally we create a circle, the circle of the earth—a Mandala, as we all know.

The one center-point—which materially does not even exist—is common to all Mandalas of all times. In it the contrasts reconcile; in it the polarity is preserved. The point is the essence of each Mandala, even though, in general, by the expression "Mandala" we mean just the opposite: the unessential, the changeable, the visible.

After all, we make this "mistake" very often: for example, when we talk about a house, we visualize its walls and the roof. But we cannot and do not even want to enter those. In fact, we are talking about the space within the walls; but that, one can neither build nor sell. Instead, one can be in it. Here we have reached a crucial point: one cannot understand more about the Mandala than the fact that the essential withdraws from the understanding—but that much one *can* understand! Understanding is tied to polarity, to space and time. Where those two end, also understanding ends. And that is exactly in the center of the Mandalas.

The external, one can also understand, for on the outside the polarity is visibly portrayed—the Christian part of the rose windows often even deals with the portrayal of the Creation (exactly the world of polarity). But in the center there is always a symbol of the Unspeakable, the ℙ for the Logos or God-Father or Christ, or in rarer cases even the T'ai Chi symbol. Each culture uses its own symbol of unity. On the following page you see a silver-piece made by Iroquois Indians.

◆ MEDITATION ◆

We now begin with a simple meditation exercise. (Therefore you don't need to know anything.) Just sit down, upright and in a comfortable position, and look at one of your colorful Mandalas, which you have set up in front of you, at eye level, a short distance away. Now you do not need to do anything else but look at the Mandala—neither especially concentrating nor straining—just look at it, focusing your eyes onto the whole Mandala. Each time, when you realize that your thoughts are wandering away from what you see, just return your consciousness to the Mandala-center. You play this game for about twenty minutes.

Wherever this meditation led you, whatever you experienced in it, it can only have been yourself or your creations that came to you. All experiences, thoughts, imaginations, dreams, and inner pictures do always reflect only ourselves.

When you repeat such exercises often, in time your interest in your own creations and your own thoughts will diminish, and you will more and more get into the center, into your own and that of the Mandala, because, after all, there is only the One.

◆ HOMELAND OF THE MANDALA ◆

The word "Mandala" is taken from the Sanskrit and is thus of Eastern origin (if one disregards for now that possibly the Brahmanistic tradition itself goes back to Druidic origins). In the consciousness of most people, Mandalas are something Eastern. As we can see in the Gothic rose windows, that didn't have to be so, because Mandalas can be found at the roots of all cultures, since they live in the roots of each human being.

In each of us the entire evolution of mankind continues—not least in the genetic code of our hereditary substance, which is the same for all living beings. After all, at the beginning of our life we start again through the millennia of the development of the physical body, even though in a shorter time: we originate as unicellular creatures, in order to then swim as water-creatures into the placenta, the fluid composition of which still corresponds to the primitive ocean. Later development contains a phase of crawling, similar to the reptiles; and finally the rising into standing position, which is as dramatic a step for each child as it probably was for mankind. Even as adults we still carry with us traces of our origin, for example in rudimentary body-hairs.

The development of language shows the same principle. As on the material level, we also carry in the soul the images and experiences from our long history—and thus we do not need to be astonished that there are also images of unity, of the paradise that we once left. The pictures of unity are Mandalas. Thus it is clear that they have to be in all human beings, and this way also in all cultures, and are our common human spiritual heritage.

ZENITH FOR MANDALAS
NADIR FOR HUMAN BEINGS

In our culture in modern times, C. G. Jung in particular worked at studying the Mandala. He found out that Mandalas appear especially in situations of acute psychic chaos (for example in cases of psychosis and acutely active neurosis). Possibly these appearances indicate a self-healing tendency of the soul in the form of spontaneous inner images. If we think of the Crusades and the Inquisition, it is also evident that Gothic architecture, with its rose windows, developed during a time of greatest outside chaos. It certainly would not be astonishing if there were, besides healing attempts in the human being (microcosm), also such endeavors of a culture or even of the world (macrocosm).

According to the maxim of Hermes Trismegistus (as above so below, as outside so inside), there is an absolute conformity between micro- and macrocosm. This may apply also to the growing interest in Mandalas, which can be observed these days, and their increasing appearance in art and meditation exercises, because once again today we are living in a time which more and more loses itself in outward appearances and leaves the souls of human beings unsatisfied. This situation is revealed in the increasing one-sidedness of our values, which in turn has to do with the one-sidedness of our thinking.

Obviously we have our brain to think, and therefore we should be able to recognize this problem within ourselves.

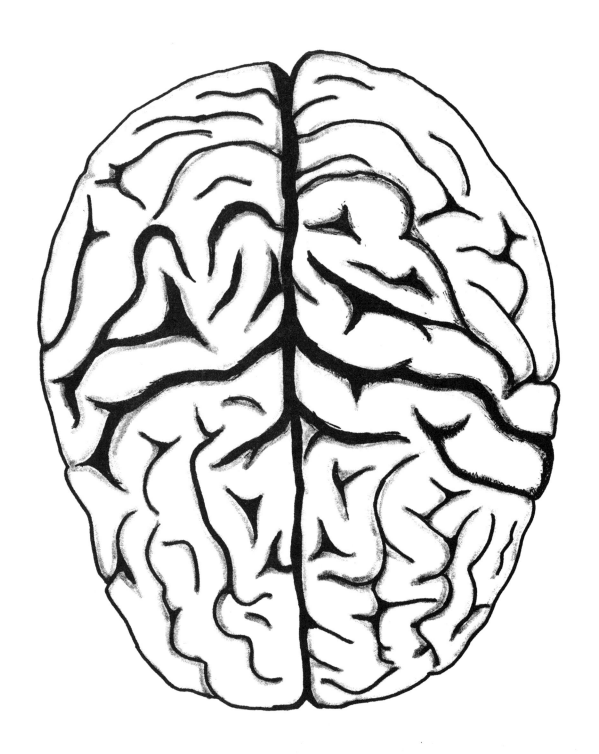

Looking at the brain from above, one is struck by at least three things:

1. It forms a kind of Mandala.
2. It is reminiscent of a labyrinth.
3. It is clearly divided into two parts and thus polar (compare with T'ai Chi signs).

In the course of time we have learned to find our way through the labyrinth of nerves of our brain. In doing so, we restricted ourselves almost exclusively to the one (namely the left) half, and through that we became one-sided. The left side is the one that thinks analytically and differentiates, that can write, read, and calculate, that on the whole dominates all functions of the intellect. In the body it rules the right side (since the nerve-streams cross in the spinal cord). The right brain-hemisphere, in turn, is responsible for one's comprehension of the world as a whole, for all artistic things, for feelings and the sensation of colors, scents, and vibrations, and for the left side of the body. One associates with it the female, the moonlike; it corresponds with the dark Yin, the negative, the magnetic, in contrast to the positive, electric, male, the light Yang of the T'ai Chi sign.

The one-sided emphasis on the brain's left half is a phenomenon that is only found in our Western civilization. American Indian cultures, for example, and for the most part Eastern cultures as well, prefer the right half. The solution for the problem, left or right—you will certainly be able to find this for yourself, after our trip into the world of the Mandalas. Yes, correct—it lies in the center!

Turning again to the brain, we will find in its depth the corpus callosum, a structure that connects both brain-halves. In this connecting structure, this center, lies the solution: i.e., to bring both halves into harmony—to experience them equally and to let them become equally important. I am convinced that the condition of enlightenment expresses itself on this level in the harmony between the two polar brain-halves. The over-utilization of either side will always be unsatisfying. In order to come to this conclusion, we need not examine the physiology of the brain. We have only to look at our world today. The West is not happy with its half, nor the East with the other one.

Also attempts of people who "cop out" show us the same. It is not a solution, when we Western, intellectually well-informed people now suddenly (out of the overwhelming certainty that it cannot go on so one-sidedly) try to go totally to the other pole and want to become hermits in India, or hobos, or Gypsies. That is not ideal either. We can see this in the people who were on this path from the beginning because they were born in a particular environment and therefore had no choice. Not that the intellect is bad or even at fault—but there is more to life than intellect. The solution lies in the center between East and West—and North and South.

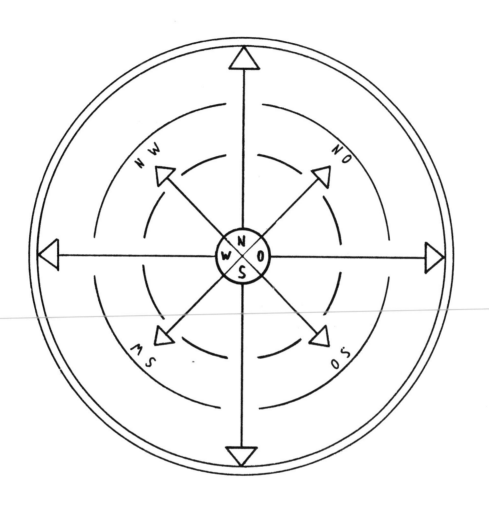

◆ ASSISTANCE IN FINDING THE CENTER ◆

In order to get to the center, to harmonize the two contrary brain-halves, it makes sense to create an environment which stimulates both hemispheres at the same time. For that we just have to look again at the traditions which meditation and religion have preserved, because for millennia they have intuitively used those scientific findings which our brain-research produces today.

At many cultic celebrations in West and East music plays an essential role and definitely has an effect on the right hemisphere. To stimulate the left one—for example, with intellectual sermons—does not make much sense, considering the dominance of the two brain-halves in our "circles." On the contrary is it good to divert the brain, to let it be active until it is tired, as for example will happen through the monotonous singing of Mantrams, but also through the reciting of the heart-prayer of the Greek Orthodox religion or of our rosary. Furthermore, scents (perfume sticks, incense) and taste (cultic meals) stimulate the right hemisphere. But above all rhythm, and each form of monotony, shifts the focal point into the direction of the center. Also a sense of vision is important for the finding of one's own center.

Thus there are no figurative portrayals at all in Islamic mosques. Yes, it is strictly forbidden for the Muslims to depict Allah or even his Prophet figuratively, and so they turn to ornamentation. But ornamentation in its monotony is definitely too boring for the left hemisphere, although its order and structure have more effect on the right hemisphere. Something similar is indicated in the Second Commandment in Exodus: "You shall not make for yourself a graven image." This warning of images has its meaning, because images allow the left hemisphere to cling to the concrete, to judge and to value.

But nevertheless the Christian religion, especially in Gothic structures, has sought concrete expression in the image-world of symbols. After all, it is possible to sink oneself (in the truest sense of the word) into the symbol. In any case, when we transform rose windows into abstract, colorful Mandalas, we do not need to mourn for the figurative depictions of the originals. Mandalas and figures, on different levels, express the same thing. Anyone who has been in a Gothic cathedral comes to understand that it is not the images that create the effect (they are much too small for that, sometimes not even recognizable from the ground), but the strange, almost magically working light shining through the windows and roses.

Think about these things and pay a little attention to your personal environment when doing your painting meditations.

MANDALA HISTORIES

Our Western industrial culture has lost the access to its roots, and thus also to its Mandalas. Even the Gothic cathedrals with their roses have been degraded from the gigantic temples that they once were to slowly dying museums, which can hardly be filled anymore with believers. As a consequence, here and there even entrance fees are being charged—this shall not be construed as criticism, but as a symbol of the fact that religion is being supplanted by commerce.

Before we even start to lament over such "godless times," we want to look at history from another, rather esoteric and thus less judgmental point of view. Also with this the Mandala can help us again, because the course of history itself has something of a Mandala. Not in vain do we talk about the "wheel of time." With the Gothic rose windows the West created one of the most highly developed expressions of the Mandala, by combining light, color, and form to create unity.

But with that, the cycle of development of the Mandala was obviously fulfilled at this spot of the world, and it first disappeared from the arts and then also from the consciousness. Gradually the universal spiritual thinking was cut into pieces and thrust aside by the rational intellectual understanding of the world. Starting in the West, the downfall of the Mandala spread over the whole world, and today exactly this thinking has led us near to the downfall of the world-Mandala.

Now, these cycles of spirituality and rationality are neither bad nor anything to fight against, but simply indications of the turn of the Mandala—most distinctly expressed in the Mandala of the tenth tarot card, that "wheel of destiny" which can also be seen on the portals and in the windows of some cathedrals. This congruity of a motif in a card game that has a deep esoteric root and the Roman Catholic church may surprise at the beginning. We will get used to it, since there are many similar parallels.

Paint this Mandala, the tenth card of the tarot game, and experience thereby what the symbol means to you.

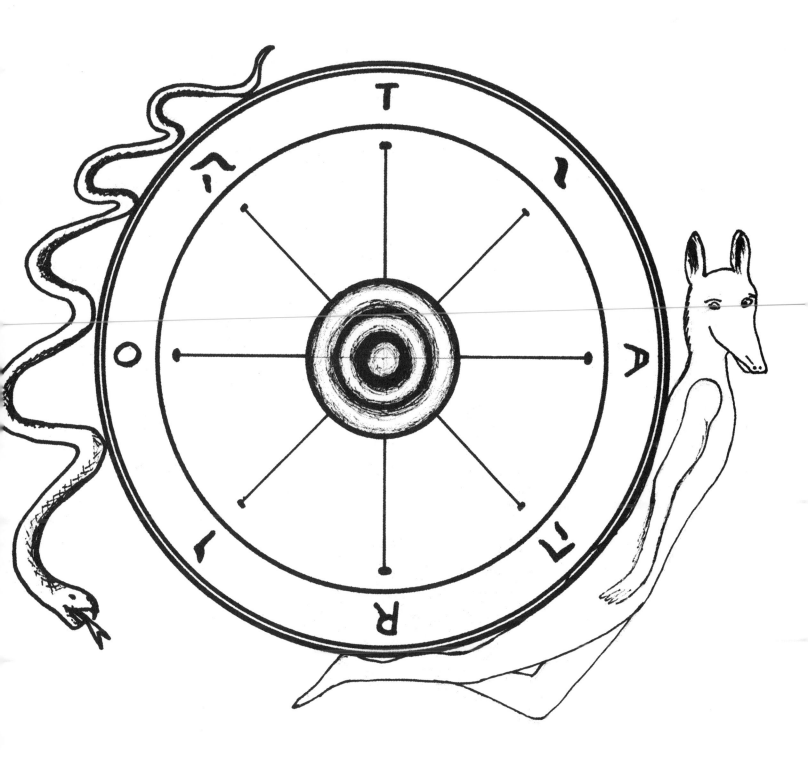

49

What does the destiny-wheel tell us?

Isn't it this?—

That everything that rises also has to descend again—and what descends will also rise again.

This is the essence of a very ancient—or rather timeless—esoteric law that is just as valid for cultures, time periods, art forms, as it is for nations, individual people—yes, even for the economic condition, trends in fashion, and tendencies in taste. This say the Mandala shows the course of history in general as well as its own destiny through time.

After its peak in the cathedrals and their roses, there began the destruction of the Mandala and thus of the serene totality by cultures marked by their "holiness." The Spanish began it with the destruction of the cultures of Central America, characteristically in search of gold, and concerned only with its external aspect. They stole it from the Aztecs, Mayans, and Incas, who were still concerned with the inner (spiritual) aspect of this most noble of all metal, symbol of their Sun God. So it should not surprise one that the Spaniards could never find this "El Dorado," this dreamlike, rich, gold country—since, after all, it is not situated in the external world. Only one who can find his inner El Dorado can also realize it in the external world. With a similar concept, which is also doomed to fail, even modern chemistry approaches alchemy and its "goldmakers."

The West agreed on its concept of conquest, and several European nations took on the destruction of entire cultures which lived under the Mandala. To look at it another way: the left half of the brain declared war on the right one, and the right half was seemingly completely defeated. But only seemingly! That can be illustrated by the timeless T'ai Chi sign.

The American Indian cultures of North America with their sand-Mandalas succumbed to the Europeans, who were united under English leadership. Although the Europeans were quite hostile among themselves, they were nevertheless in agreement in their effort to strike against the cultures oriented to the whole in North and South America. Also on the other continents the spiritual cultures had no chance against the new thinking and acting. This way the Mandala was also defeated in India, where it had traditionally determined the entire life. Characteristically, one of the symbols of liberation in our century was again the wheel—that spinning wheel that Mahatma Gandhi turned incessantly to lead the Indians back to their own beliefs. So the Indians had to twist for themselves the thread that connects them with the roots of their tradition.

The subjection of Tibet by China put a certain end to the destruction of the Mandala cultures. China was motivated by Western rationalistic ideology; its old culture, characterized by Taoism and its symbol, the T'ai Chi, had already succumbed to the new thinking. In Tibet the Mandalas had played a role which dominated the entire life.

Now the living Mandalas in Europe, America, Africa, Australia, and Asia were destroyed, or their corpses were carried off into museums. This desecration happened worldwide. Even at the Mandala's origin, in Europe, the cathedrals decayed to sight-seeing buildings; for example, the labyrinth of Chartres was cramped with chairs, on which the followers of a torpid religion listened to rational sermons which only seldom touched the center anymore.

The Mandala of the world had taken on the form shown here.

But the Mandalas never died completely. They survived in the shadow, in the ruins, fantasies, giving vent to their emotions in madness and drug-excesses. They even crept into their counter-world of technology, the most important symbol of which became the wheel in the gear unit—the cogwheels of industry. No wonder that many people in our culture feel like a very small wheel in an immense, anonymous machine.

We do not need to fear for the Mandalas. They cannot perish, as long as at least **one** person survives. And even if the one half (of the brain or of the T'ai Chi sign) dominates ever so strongly, in its own center the antipode always survives as well (the black point in the white field).

This development into one-sidedness is neither good nor bad—it **is.** It has its roots in the Mandala itself, and it was predicted by Mandala-cultures (for example, in the visions of the American Indian prophet Black Elk, and in the prophecies of the Hopis, which predict the path of events of the American Indian nations up to their destruction).

Today we are at a turning point, at the point of the rediscovery of our roots, of our internal Mandalas. Also that is neither good nor bad—it **is.** So we experience gradually, and not accidentally, a revival of the Mandalas in the external (world), in the arts and in the traditions of meditations, which are waking up to a new life. We can read this development in **each** Mandala; it is our duty. We now meet our shadow, and the shadow becomes our task. The search (which had stopped completely in the external world, stuck there in addiction and desperation, precisely in the polarity) is turning again inward to the center, to the middle, to the meditation. The circle of the Mandala closes once again, in order to open up again and to close again and to open again. . . .

◆ SACRIFICE ◆

Now we want to do an exercise, one in which we observe ourselves making peace with the downfall and the destruction, and therefrom possibly waking up to a new reality. Before you paint the next Mandala, let yourself know that you will subsequently destroy it. Observe yourself when imagining this, and also later when painting. Especially pay attention to the intellect and its ideas. Listen to it when it whispers to you something like the following: "A ritual of sacrifice, obviously—what antiquated nonsense!" Or: "We'll do that now very quickly; it is anyway just for—well, actually, for whom? In any case not for me!" Or: "That is totally pointless, it's dangerous—forget it!" Or even more clever: "I won't dream of ruining the nice book, when there is already so much work invested in it . . ." Or in general: "On principle I do not participate in something like that!"

If your intellect has gone this far, then be pleased. Let it have its decision, and then make the sacrifice without intellect. You will see it is possible! It is even more effective without intellect, since now you are rid of all performance pressures and of all thoughts of effectivity at the same time.

And then you begin. Do this with love, instead of with intellect.

And here is another chance:

You had intended to keep theory and practice together and not to read ahead. Now is an especially good moment to stick to this intention—to practice being faithful to yourself. Therefore now paint this Mandala, conscious of its subsequent sacrifice. Only when it is finished go to the instruction of the execution of the sacrifice.

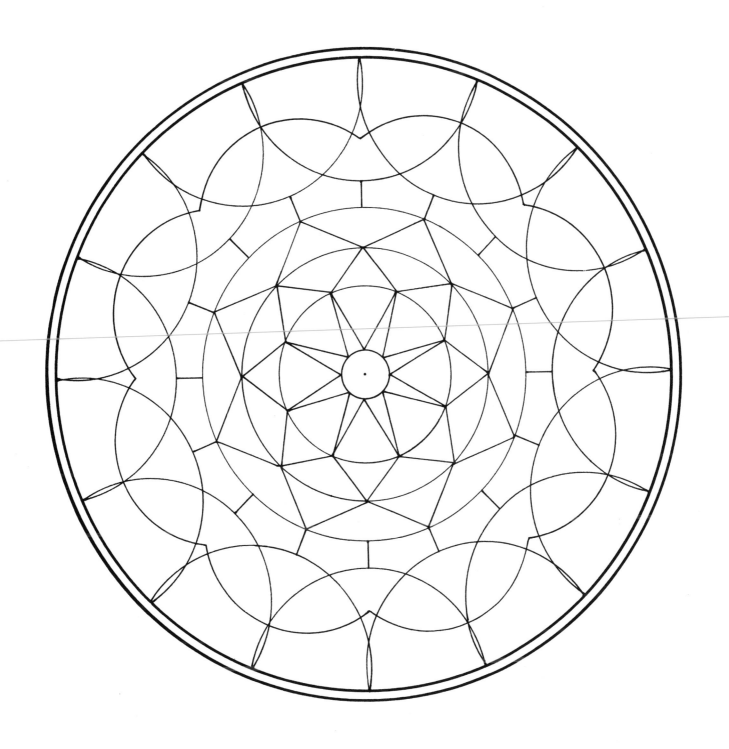

✦ BURNING RITUAL ✦

Now, employing sensible precautions in the use of fire, burn the Mandala (from page 57) in the following manner:

1. Be conscious of yourself and of all thoughts and sensations that arise now.

2. Tune yourself into the ritual character of this act—since it is a sacrifice, after all—maybe by concentrating beforehand on each Mandala, which from now on will live on only in you, since you will destroy its external form.

3. Take a stick of incense, light it, and with it burn through the center of the Mandala.

4. Now take a lit candle and hold the page, with your Mandala on it, up so that it is apart as much as possible from all other pages. Set the Mandala on fire from the back, exactly at the small hole in the center.

5. Let only the Mandala burn almost up to its outer border, and then blow out the flames!
   All right—begin!

When we sacrifice a Mandala we have to be aware that it is impossible to destroy its true essence. We can merely free it from its materialistic and thus stiff form and give it back to its origins. The Navajo Indians follow the same principle when they let their sand-Mandala "drift away into sand" again, according to the ritual ceremony. The true form, according to their point of view, has itself united long ago with the respective human being, animal, or God.

In the end, destruction does not exist at all. A Mandala can no more die than a human being—the essence merely changes its level. Now, you do not need to destroy each Mandala physically—although just the returning of the Mandala into unity can become a nice ritual. For once you do something really free of judgment, for yourself alone, without reservations. . . . The Ego will slowly become tired of resisting this idea.

On the other hand, it can be just as nice to preserve the completed Mandalas and to enjoy them. In Tibet, for example, Mandalas are not destroyed, but brought into ritual-rooms, where they convey a solemn atmosphere, serving as a focus for meditation and as objects for concentration.

Of course you too can treat your Mandalas with a similar respect—or just consider them to be colorful pictures. Somewhere in between these extremes you will recognize your own emotions. Allow yourself to feel honestly, to feel what is true for you. The point here is certainly not a pretense of holiness, it is not outward holiness. If you were not able to let yourself go, because you were, for example, just too proud of your work, then also allow that to yourself. It is really all right—because it **is.**

Again and again we all fall for the great illusion, that desperate hope to be able to steal something from the whole piece for our Ego, something that belongs only to us and excludes everybody else. It is an expression of illusion, to be able to keep something for ourselves, an obvious denial of the only security which we have, that certainty that we have to free ourselves from everything when we will free ourselves from our body.

Now you have performed this ritual once and thus made a classical burnt offering on the altar of your Ego. If you haven't done it, or if you have first read on to this page, you missed something essential, which you can only catch up on with difficulty. And it is just as well, because this is how it is. In this case take your time for another exercise. Ask yourself how well in your life you can rely on your resolutions, how much your intellect dominates you—how it is always a bit smarter and that way so "surely" leads you past the essential. Ask if you want that this way.

If you experienced difficulties with the sacrifice-exercise, repeat the ritual at least one more time. Bring to your mind, during the act of burning, the realization that everything is transitory in this polar world—including our bodies. Also we can only go back there, where we came from, just like the burning Mandala before us.

How difficult it is to really take back one's own creations you see at your burnt page. There is now, left behind, in place of your colorful Mandala, a carbonized circle with a hole in the center—a different kind of Mandala. It is really difficult to get back something which was once created—and that does not only hold true for Mandalas.

From page 57 a Mandala can be seen through the carbonized hole. It is the west rose of Notre Dame de Paris, and it depicts the reversed process: the Creation of the world. Now turn to this Mandala and create your own world in color.

The thought that everything is (as it is) in order is very old, but very hard for us to accept. We actually did not need a new point of view, but a new way to observe, in order to see the natural result of a new beginning out of destruction and downfall. In the original Greek the word catastrophe actually means "turning-back" (hé katastrophé). According to that, the ancients obviously saw in each catastrophe also a chance to turn back.

To the same degree today a catastrophe tells us that it is time now to turn back, to move out of the extreme into the direction of the center. That we, following the law of the pendulum, will end up again in other extremes, we can already see in the tenth tarot card, the wheel of destiny. Both—the pendulum as well as the wheel—show us the same way out: only in the center is peace forever. The pendulum (if it is not being driven by a clockwork constantly energized) will lose a little energy with each swing and finally find peace in the center.

Now we want to move the emphasis even more distinctly from the head to the hands, to manual labor. This path is by no means new. On the whole, there is nothing new written in this entire book; everything was here before: it stems from somewhere. You can decide now: "He stole it," or "He has busily collected it." Or you can just take it as what it is, as frame for your path. And do not forget, each frame is a restriction and in the end has to be broken.

The combination of intellectual and manual labor we already find in the old monk's rule: *Ora et labora*—pray and work! This rule stems from a time when the monks were the bearers of culture and thus were also the architects of the Christian churches. Many spiritual teachers were and are concerned with the combination of handwork and headwork. We may think, for example, of the Freemasons whose organization was developed by builders and who created as well an essential basis of modern culture.

Some rules for the manual labor and the proper attitude toward it: We are primarily concerned with the work itself, only secondarily with the result. (Attention: the intellect will try to reverse this!)

There is nothing to succeed in or to accomplish, and there is above all no time limit by which you have to succeed or accomplish something. And if you then, nevertheless, succeed in something, or also accomplish something even faster or slower, something even more beautiful or uglier than your friend does, then that does not make you any better or worse. It **is**. Above all, it is allowed to be.

You can learn the ideal attitude from the birds when they build their nests. They are not in a particular hurry, yet they do not linger; they do it neither sloppily, nor precisely, in an exaggerated manner. They do it at the right time, and not in competition with their partner, but together with him.

They take the path in the middle, and they do it out of their center.

Now paint your bird-nest Mandala with this attitude: blade for blade.

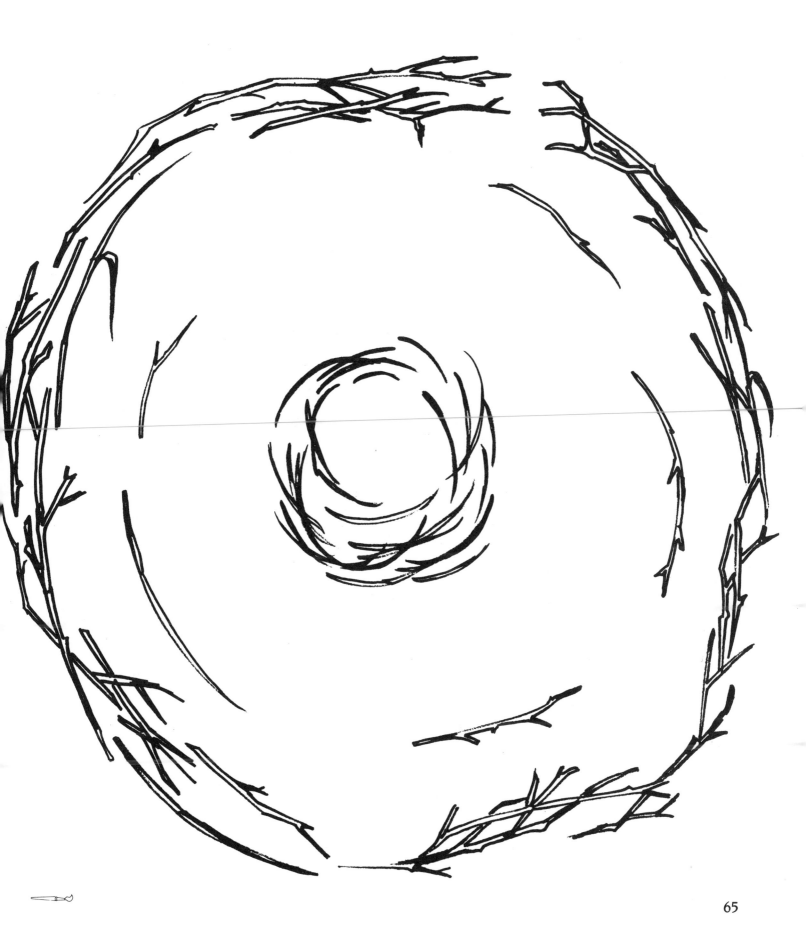

THE DANCE AROUND THE CENTER— AND THE INTELLECT AS SPECTATOR

The best help to feel one's own center while acting is to stay conscious; no matter what might happen; no matter what one does at any time, to watch oneself consciously. To watch oneself when one becomes impatient, to watch oneself when it becomes boring (the intellect lives on diversion, and "boring" is one of its favorite arguments), to watch oneself when one becomes furious, and to watch oneself when one gets tired. . . . Make it clear to yourself again and again that the issue is a meditation, and that at best this is to be compared with a prayer. Who would want to pray especially well or fast or accurately or effectively! Our sole goal is the center.

Let's have a look at activities that work only when they are executed out of the center: e.g., the work at a potter's wheel. The wheel turns at high speed, and the work can succeed only when it is executed exactly in the center and out of absolute calmness. Otherwise the lump of clay will inevitably fall off the wheel. The potter calls this activity "centering."

We experience a similar phenomenon in the Eastern fighting techniques. The high speed and the force of the movements and hits depend on the calmness in the center of the fighter. It is also the sought-after experience in the T'ai Chi—that feeling that the entire body moves but one remains at the same time unmoved; that all movement flows from the center, and the center nevertheless is in calmness.

Similar to the feeling for the body in T'ai Chi may be the feeling for the flute, when sounds swing through it, which it does not produce and which nevertheless come out of it.

Also the whirling dance of the Islamic dervishes shows us this principle. They spin and whirl in order to find in their center the calmness (Allah, God). There is something else this dance around our own center can show us, which we likewise experience with our most timeless dance, the waltz. If we do not succeed in finding this center at least approximately, so long as the intellect tries to guide us as well, we become hopelessly dizzy. Only when the intellect gives up do we overcome the dizziness and then we can spin around almost without limit. With the dance that has no intention, we still succeed relatively easily in leaving the intellect out of it for a short period of time and to spin around self-forgettingly with the music. That's why dancing is so much fun for those who reach this level. Just try the opposite: to dance correctly and well. Our self-forgetfulness, actually an Ego-forgetfulness, leaves us quickly.

At our painting game we can succeed in leaving the intellect out of it, only we first must learn how to play again.

Create this fantasy-Mandala with colors which correspond to its inner dynamics (for example, fiery red shades).

◆ THE WHEEL ◆

It is not only dances that show the principle of the movement around the resting center; so do the centuries-old rose windows of Gothic architecture. In contrast to their external movement, there is the calmness of the centerpoint. At its most radical we find this principle in a cyclone. In the center of the cyclone an almost sinister calmness prevails, surrounded by enormously powerful dynamics. We may clarify this image most simply by observing a common wheel. The conscious learning of the wheel principle might (like the standing upright) also have been an important achievement of awakening mankind.

The ancient human being had thus succeeded in taking an outstanding step, comparable to making fire or to working with metal. The human being was probably relatively early aware of the godly (or perfected) character of the wheel as symbol, since he much earlier prayed to the sun as a God. Maybe he even built his wheel following the pattern of the sun-wheel. In any case he now had also on earth a sun symbol.

There is various evidence of the fact that the circle was a very early symbol of the divine (e.g., compare the sun calendar of the Aztecs). Thus already the Cro-Magnon people, who lived in the French Arriège Valley long before our chronology, probably chose a cave to be their temple (reaching it only with very great difficulty), because having a natural dome, it was round as a circle (cave of Niaux).

Even much later the windows of churches were still built in a round shape, while in unconsecrated buildings this form remained an exception. Also many basilicas and almost all Greek Orthodox temples adhere to this distinction. The church house (on the earth) is square, but the dome (which reaches towards the sky) is round. In the Eastern cultures this distinction in the symbolism is also very clear: the square stands for the material (polar) world; the circle is the divine form, which is committed to unity.

Create the simple wheel-window of the Cathedral of Burgos.

• THE WORLD OF ROSE WINDOWS— SYMBOLISM THAT COMBINES TIMES AND CULTURES •

If we remember the universality of the Mandala symbol and bring to mind that there is only one truth and thus only one source from which all religions draw, then today's practices of limitation, exclusion, and degradation of others among the religions strike us as surprising. Even though our Christian church today strongly opposes alchemy, it is still obvious that old churches are full of alchemistic symbols.

If astrology is supposed to be a "devilish superstition," why then are there so many astrological symbols in the cathedrals? Yes, almost every second Gothic window-rose is based on the twelfth key and contains the portrayal of the twelve signs of the zodiac.

Is it really "coincidence" that the universally depicted symbols of the four evangelists exactly correspond to the fixed cross of the zodiac: lion, eagle (as redeemed Scorpio), angel (Aquarius), and Taurus, and that these now "accidentally" symbolize exactly the four elements of the ancients (fire, water, air, earth)? Hardly! It is reasonable to assume that the builders and planners of the early churches—and especially of the cathedrals—knew more than their administrators of today.

We want to try to find the connection to this early knowledge and to investigate the unity in its diversity. That's what the word "uni-verse" means, after all, and the university was probably originally the place where these laws were supposed to be realized. Today the left brain-hemisphere is content with the "versity," the diversity. On our trip through the world of the rose windows we will touch on the most different cultures, times, and systems, with the one goal: to track down the unity in the diversity, to dissolve the apparent contrast between these two terms, and thereby to find our path back.

Lao-tse says: "The capability to recognize the source of the ancient knowledge is called the 'red thread,' which leads along the path."

Create the wheel of destiny of the tenth tarot card on the portal of the Cathedral of Beauvais.

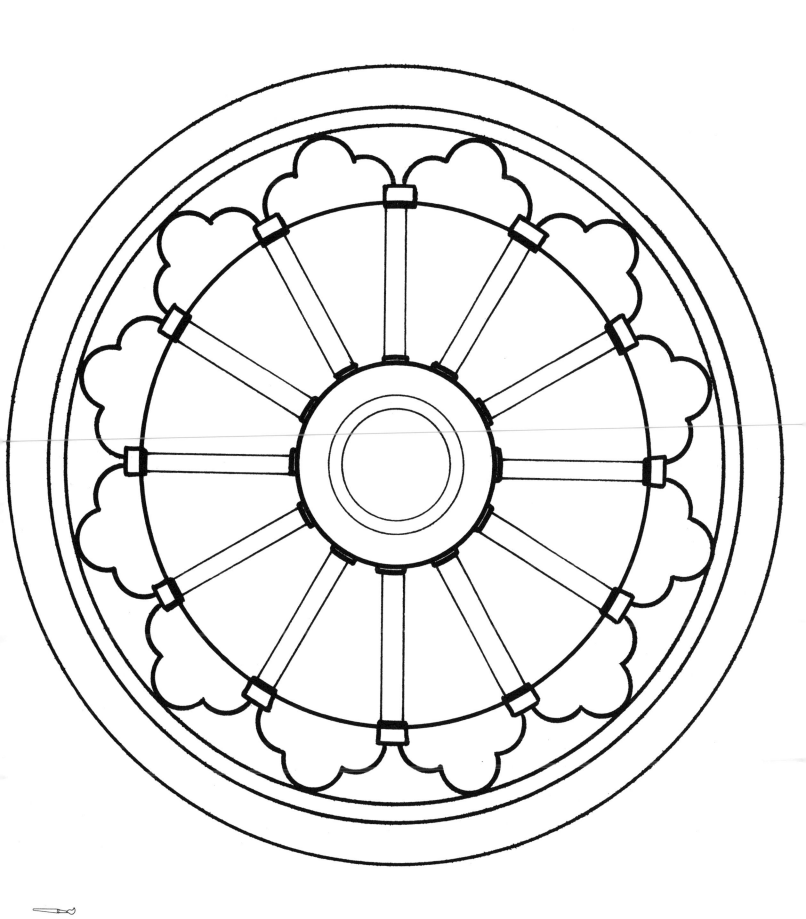

The combination of square (as symbol for the limited) and circle (as standard symbol for the unlimited) corresponds with the structure of the Yantras of the East.[1] We find the same combination in Islamic tradition; we find it as well on the portals of the cathedrals, especially in the roses. If we look at the south-rose of Clermont-Ferrand, we will see how it expresses the unlimited (circle) in the frame of the limited (square), and for that it uses pure ornamentation, which could very easily have originated from Islamic art.

---

1. The Mandalas, which are used for religious rituals in India, Tibet, and Nepal, are still today called Yantras. In a small way (e.g., as painted meditational aids) as also in a big way (e.g., as ground plans for temples) these draw the connection between the divine (circle or point) and the material world (square).

In the west-rose of Notre Dame de Paris (which you have already painted on page 59), the Virgin Mary with the child is surrounded by twenty-four fields, which in nice harmony contain the twelve signs of the zodiac, the virtues and vices and the prophets.

Some Christian saints carry strange tools with them, which are easily recognized as alchemistic implements; as, for example, the patriarchs of the Revelation in the Cathedral of Santiago de Compostela.

On a relief in the Spanish cloister and pilgrimage church San Juan de la Peña one can clearly recognize an Athanor and an alchemist's oven. The north-rose of Notre Dame de Paris is still today called the alchemist-rose.

In the Cathedral of Lyon we find the symbol of the T'ai Chi in the center, i.e., exactly where it belongs according to Taoistic philosophy. It is surrounded by twenty-four patriarchs of the Apocalypse.

A rose of the Cathedral of Toulouse also shows us a symbol very similar to the T'ai Chi and provides perhaps another hint. In the center this rose contains depictions of the Templar Cross. Possibly a key to the understanding of the still mysterious origin of the cathedrals and their secret symbolism is concealed by the Templars. Even today it is unexplained how the Gothic, in such short time (about 100 years), could bring about such a wealth of enormous buildings. No phase of preparation is now evident; no failed attempts are known to us; no development towards the Gothic has been discovered. Furthermore, most of these cathedrals are situated in settled areas that are still small today, but at the time of construction were certainly unable solely to provide money and knowledge for the execution of such buildings.

The Templars, on the other hand, owned at that time, excluding the papacy, the most influential and powerful organization in the Occident. Furthermore, Occident and Orient, although opposite each other as enemies at the beginning, later on were probably more and more opposites which positively influenced each other.

81

We find the wheel of destiny at various places and in different depictions. Cowen,[2] who dedicated a wonderful book to the rose windows, found out that during the same time the "wheel of happiness," as he called it, was developing into the Gothic rose, the zodiac signs were becoming the symbols of the evangelists. Thus it always is: the old contents are being made over into the new form and externally adapt to it. According to this principle, Christian temples sprang up on the site of old Druidic places of worship; old pilgrimage roads such as the one to Santiago de Compostela were given new Christian meaning. At the wheel of destiny in the façade of Beauvais, the typical symbolism of the tenth tarot key is portrayed, whereas before, the Egyptian figures were dressed in Occidental garments.

In addition to the Gothic designs, we find other symbolism which combines cultures in our churches. Let's think of the symbolism of the simply structured wheel windows of Romanticism and of the wheel of rebirth of Buddhism. In the center of this wheel lies the Redemption, often portrayed by the thousand-petaled Lotus, which grows out of the head of the Buddha. Also in the center of the Christian wheel window lies the Redemption, here often portrayed by a flower: the rose, the sign of Mary and thus of love; or by the Logos, the Christ. A wonderful example for that is our next Mandala, the one of the west façade of the fourteenth-century Cathedral of Orvieto, in the center of which, in the midst of ornaments, the head of Christ is depicted. The Mandala is here again surrounded by a square. In the outer fields are fifty-two heads, which probably represent the weeks of the year.

This wheel has another special feature: twenty-two steps. That is an important number to the ancients, since there are exactly twenty-two tarot keys (major arcana) and twenty-two letters in the Hebrew alphabet, both of which play an important role in the Kabbala.

Again and again we find the same symbols leading us to the same source. Even our already highly developed alphabet still consists of letters (lit.: Buchstabe = book-sticks, or also beech-tree-sticks); those linguistically still refer to the beech twigs that the ancient Teutons and their ancestors employed in reading the will of the gods. In fact, these beech twigs originally were not a system of information among people, but a divinatory system, in which the priest of the tribe threw the sticks and from the way they landed read God's will (using the same principle, the Taoists throw the yarrow sticks of the *I Ching*).

On our path through the world of symbols of the roses it can only be helpful to learn anew to pay attention to the letters, in order to unravel the Creation in their structures.

2. Cowen Painton. *Rose Windows of the Gothic Cathedrals*. Freiburg: Herder, 1979.

Our next exercise leads us now into a cathedral, since, after all, these gigantic testimonies of our Occidental past are still standing in our midst. It is certainly not by coincidence that they are strongly protected. Even such radical movements as the French Revolution have not succeeded, in the end, in seriously damaging the cathedrals. The relatively minor damages are still visible today. It would have been easy enough to throw stones into the "holy" windows, yet, despite all the antireligious hate, no one threw stones.

For me, the fate of the Cathedral of Cologne is most impressive. When I was a child, my father showed me a picture of the completely bombed-out city of Cologne. I was startled by the fact that the huge, black cathedral towered out of the desert of ruins almost undamaged. My feeling at that time was a conflict between: "A guardian angel, after all?" and that there had to be something fishy about it. Whichever explanation the individual might accept, these monumental structures still stand and cannot be overlooked.

Why don't you visit a cathedral which is close to you. In the nave, you then sit down in such a way that you face a rose. Once you have found your place in the church, simply let your eyes wander over the rose and keep your attention on it as a whole. The point is not to recognize something specific, but to behold. This way your gaze will relax completely without your doing anything. Let then happen what happens by itself; and if nothing happens, then that seems to be the best thing at the moment.

Repeat this exercise in front of the rose window once again at another time of the day, and pay attention, while doing that, how each time of the day changes the creations that are revealed in the window. This way you can now also experience the creation of the rose window in the colors of the morning and those of the evening.

On the next two pages you will find the same rose. Paint it at first in the colors of the morning, and on the opposite page, in those of the evening.

If you were able to do this exercise actually in a cathedral, you would notice that it is built according to the light. The central aisle points exactly from west to east, and the side aisle forms the short beam of the Latin cross from north to south. That is not a coincidence. Almost all cathedrals are oriented in this way: i.e., point to the East (Lat. *oriens:* The East, the morning, the Sun-God). Traditionally the altar stood at the crossing-point of the two beams of the cross and thus in the center, as you may see in Chartres, so the transformation, the revelation of the secret, could take place in that area of the unlimited, the divine. This is because the cross originated out of the Mandala, which we can nicely see at the compass rose (page 45) and at the symbol of the rose-cross.

Why, we can ask ourselves, are the Christian churches oriented like that? Yes, why do we in the West actually use such a verb as "orient," which, after all, does not indiscriminately mean "to look for the direction," but literally means "to point toward the east." Maybe because the ancient esoteric wisdom, *ex orient lux,* which we can still observe each morning in the sky, is also valid for the Christian religion? Obviously so, even if nowadays hardly any priest attaches importance to that.

Thus the cathedrals still contain many elements of an order which is barely known to us. For example, most roses follow the exact cardinal points in their theme; in the West lies the future, so portrayed by the Last Judgment, Christ as the judge of the worlds or of the construction of the New Jerusalem; pointing East there is no rose, but the choir. The East is already present in the center of each rose in the nonexistence of space and time. Because if we think of time as being linear, a straight line, the so-called time-axle that coming from the past leads into the future, so we will see that the present moment, the so-called point of time, does not have any expansion on the time-axle; it is, so to say, time-less.

Just as it did before for the space, the Mandala now (in this case the rose) reveals time as being an illusion. In the outside, in the spheres of the rose it is portrayed as we perceive it out of our polarity—in the most different pictures: the seasons, the twelve months, the fifty-two weeks of the year, the zodiac. But all that comes together and unites itself in the center-point, and in this way disappears from the time-axle. While outside the Creation dominates, following the laws of the wheel of destiny through time, in the center the Logos dominates, Christ from eternity to eternity.

And the rose teaches us one other phenomenon which is connected with time: While outside in the polarity of the Creation everything develops itself and moves incessantly (ηάντα ρεῖ—everything flows, as Heraclitus stated it), the center remains in timeless, eternal peace. The conclusion for us is: The only certainty in our polar world is that nothing remains as it is. Only when we have returned to the center will we realize that everything remains as it is: eternal, timeless.[3]

---

3. We find in our physical environment a complete analogy to this situation. We know that this world, in the last analysis, consists of atoms; and that these atoms actually consist primarily of energy: i.e., the substance-portion is incredibly small and lies in the center. We live strongly embedded in our world of illusion, an empty world. The only thing that really is is completely in the center, and we never come in contact with that. That which we do come in contact with is demonstrably illusion.

When Christ, reigning in the center of the rose, states, "Nobody comes to the Father, except through me," that means to us: There is only one way to heaven or to God, and that way leads through the one center of the timeless and spaceless unity, back to that Eden where Adam and Eve did not realize yet that they were different (man and woman: polar), because in the unity there is no differentiation.

Also in the words of Christ, here is a complement to his statement quoted above: "Because truly I tell you: the kingdom of heaven is in you!" Looking at it from this point of view, the rose window, just as any other Mandala, becomes a map—a map not only of the entire universe, but also of our inner soul-landscape. Then it does not astonish one anymore that this same map appears again and again as sign and symbol, and everywhere is being recognized by the inner nature of each person. This symbol has always been there and will always remain, since it exists on all levels.

Also, as we have seen in our short discourse of history, it cannot be banished from this earth. It will always rise up again from the depth of the soul, even if we want ever so much to push it back there—just as the fairy tales and legends of the nations will regenerate themselves again and again out of these depths. There is no escape from the sphere of the Mandala. The circle will always close up again, as much as we might fight against it. Whatever we do to the Mandala, it will always appear again; we will always recognize it again, be it at the tail unit of a fighter-bomber or in the Star of Bethlehem, on the cap of a revolutionary or in the rose of Notre Dame.

Even if we turn it counterclockwise, which runs against the order (as happened with the Swastika, the old runic sign), it is in the nature of the wheel of destiny that "above" has to become "below" again, and vice versa. And in fact a small, balancing counter-force, which pulls back to the center, arose with the symbol of the white rose under the Swastika at the time of its strongest deployment of power.

. . . Automatically one remembers the antipodal white point in the black field of the T'ai Chi sign.

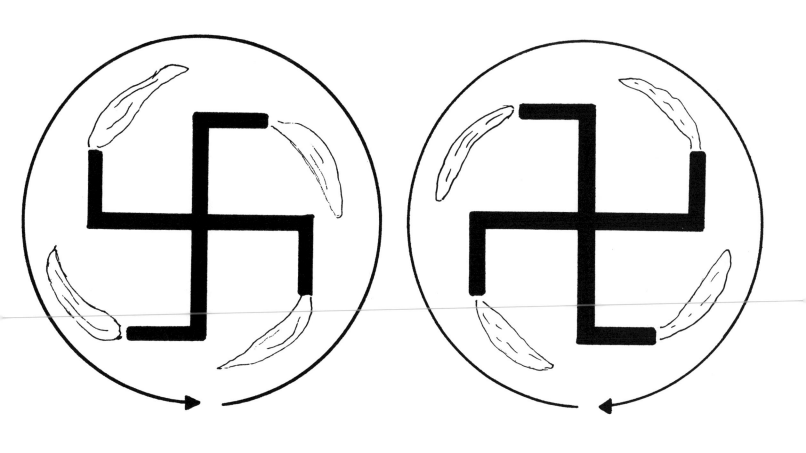

If we let the fire come out of the open ends of the swastika, we will have the Indian fire-wheel, which in this case rotates to the left and symbolizes the chaotic, destructive forces.

This sun-wheel rotates clockwise and symbolizes thus the cosmic, constructive forces.

In the center of Gothic window rosettes are revealed the two big secrets of our existence: space and time. So they remind us of another Mandala that also connects space and time to a symbol: the horoscope, that space-time equation which is computed using the birthplace and birth time of a person or of an event. Now, a horoscope is not a stiff, immutable construction, as some may assume, but is instead, like each Mandala, a dynamic process. Only in the center there is peace, and it is a long way to get there. It is best to imagine yourself as a spiral which gets narrower as it becomes taller (like a snail shell). Once you have traversed the circle it begins anew, only at a slightly higher level, becoming somewhat smaller each time, and this way one gradually approaches the center, and thus the Redemption (compare the Buddhistic wheel of rebirth, and the pendulum).

We can consider the rose window as being the horoscope of the world. It portrays equally the birth of the world and its further development (just like a horoscope).

Now paint this ancient depiction of the horoscope-Mandala in colors that, if the idea appeals to you, correspond with the individual spheres and planets.

In case you have not studied astrological symbolism so far, here are some brief hints.

The twelve signs of the zodiac are assigned to the four elements.

The three fire signs are: Aries - Leo - Sagittarius
The three earth signs are: Taurus - Virgo - Capricorn
The three air signs are: Gemini - Libra - Aquarius
The three water signs are: Cancer - Scorpio - Pisces

Out of this alone results a certain coordination of colors. A further differentiation is possible, if you also take into consideration the planet which coordinates with each sign of the zodiac.

Mars (red) to	Aries,
Venus (green) to	Taurus,
Mercury (yellow) to	Gemini,
Moon (silver) to	Cancer,
Sun (gold) to	Leo,
Mercury (orange) to	Virgo,
Venus (green) to	Libra,
Pluto (dark-red) to	Scorpio,
Jupiter (lilac) to	Sagittarius,
Saturn (black) to	Capricorn,
Uranus (blue and multicolored) to	Aquarius, and
Neptune (bottle-green) to	Pisces.

These color assignments are somewhat disputed, but that does not matter for our purpose. Pick the coordination which feels the most agreeable to you.

93

In the rose window, the birth of the world resembles an explosion; and thus probably it also resembles that original explosion which the world of science has dubbed "the big bang." The light explodes into all its aspects: it becomes colorful and radiant; it becomes harder and harder towards the edge, in order to finally consolidate into stone. Conversely, the rose at the same time is taking back the Creation and collecting it in a point, just like a convex lens, whose beams, focused on a point, can kindle a fire.

Some roses, in fact, have at their outer edge structures that look as if they were burnt with a burning-glass, which concentrate the light onto the center, as for example the south-rose of Chartres, where twelve such burning-glasses direct the light to the center. The central medallion has once more these twelve burning-glasses, whereby Christ, there portrayed, in the truest sense of the word becomes the burning-point of the universe: He redeems us there from the wheel of destiny, just as the emptiness of Nirvana redeems the Buddhist from the wheel of rebirth.

Light is a central phenomenon of the roses and one of the secrets of the Gothic. Even today the glass of these arched windows and of the roses has kept its secret, and despite many attempts, no one has ever succeeded in creating similarly brilliant colored glass. Some few techniques have been duplicated, but the last secrets remained undiscovered, as with so many other secrets of the Gothic. It is said that in the thirteenth century gemstones were cast into the glass of the windows, in order to catch even more light in them, since the secret of gems is not only to let the light in, but also through its special qualities to refract, to scarcely release it again, so that light remains caught in the stone and makes it sparkle.

The rose windows display a similar phenomenon—through them the light bursts in, almost as through gems, and immerses the inside of the cathedral in strongly mystical light. Thus the windows turn into the stars of the cathedral and the roses into a level of mediation between the actual sun and the person inside the cathedral. The rose window interprets for us the sun, into the light of which we can hardly look directly, just as little as we can directly bear God's presence. The same applies to the Logos, which forms the center of many rose windows, the mediator between us and God's infinity.

Like stars, which sparkle in the nave of the cathedral, high above the human beings, the rose windows lead the way, just like the Star of Bethlehem led the way for the three wise men from the East. And they still light up the same way—leading to Christ, the Logos. Also the Star of David, the six-pointed star that unites the macrocosm with the microcosm (often portrayed by two triangles that interpenetrate each other: fire and water, red and blue, the main colors of the rose windows), announces the birth of the light at the time of the winter solstice (the greatest darkness) just as the rose windows announced their message at a time of greatest darkness.

Now create the star of the dome of the Cathedral of Burgos.

THE WORLD OF COLORS

The history of the Creation begins with the words "Let there be light." Thus from the beginning the light is central. Without light, nothing would be revealed to us. The rose window is the light of the cathedral; it is the rose window that brings the cathedral into existence and the rose window is itself also an image of the Creation. Emerging out of the center is a world of colors and structures that become more and more material toward the outside and finally lead to the stony wall-structure of the cathedral.

In the same manner that out of the spaceless point all space grows, the entire world comes into being out of the one white light, in the colors and forms of which we constantly lose our way.

The illumination lent by the rose points us to the essential in the center, the Logos, just as the essential of the cathedral is the inner space, and by no means the stony walls and towers—even if we, tired of being drawn in many directions, think of forms and structures when we speak of the cathedral. But the essence never lies in the form, it always lies behind it. The form merely exists to guide us to the Essential. Thus also in the wheel, the center (the actual essential, the hub) is empty—and still in the truest sense of the word everything is contained in it and turns around it.

And so the essential of the rose also lies in its center, in that "golden center" of St. Thomas Aquinas, in the Logos, in that idea which rests behind the central image. Everything that grows out of this center belongs to the "world of the ten thousand things," that creation behind which one is supposed to rediscover the One. Here the roses of the cathedral help us, because as, on the one hand, they divert the light, on the other hand they also catch the eye and lead it back, as if on its own, into the middle, to the Essential, and hold it there in the center.

So like all the nice things of the world, which captivate us in the true sense of the word, colors belong to the world of forms and illusions. They buoy up a picture of abundance but meanwhile they are only an expression of deficiency—an expression of the lack of light. The all-embracing unity is in the center, where there is no color— but towards the outside begins the world of polarity. In our perception everything is determined by contrast—by the missing pole: something is small because something else is big; something there is hot, because somewhere else it is cold; good needs bad, beautiful needs ugly, rich needs poor, man needs woman; and even Christ needs in our world an antipode, the devil, and He respects him as the "master of this our material world."

Consequently, each color has its anti-color, namely the one that it lacks in order to become white again. Thus does a single color actually always need all the others, in order to produce white again. Somewhat simplified, each color has a complementary color, together with which it becomes almost white (in practice rather grey). So if an object is red, that means that it lacks green and, vice versa. If something looks blue to us, it lacks yellow, etc.

In order to further familiarize ourselves with the nature of colors, we want to do some exercises.

That all colors come out of white, and therefore white contains all other colors, you can see when you let the light of the sun or even that of a light bulb fall onto a prism. If that is too complicated for you, you only have to think of a rainbow (which too is a natural Mandala). The rainbow is created because the (white) sunlight refracts in the innumerable raindrops. You can make that clear to yourself one more time with the following Mandala.

Colorize each field with the indicated color!

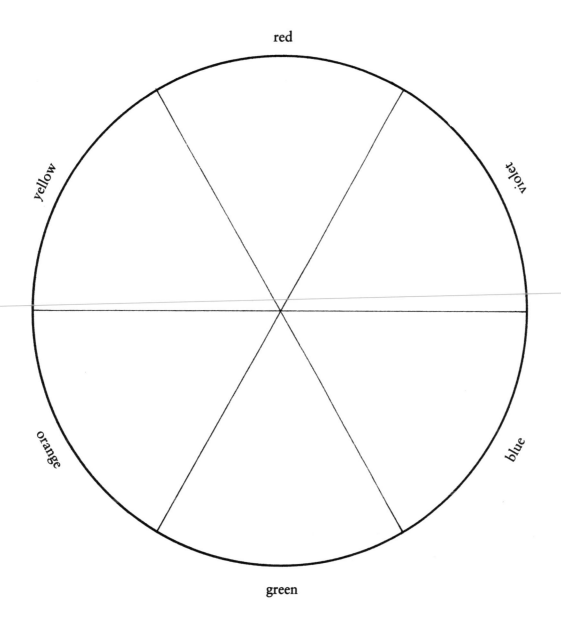

Now if you feel like it, you can let all these rainbow colors become white again. For that you do not need a lot of magic, you just have to do a little work. Draw again such a color-circle-Mandala and cut it out, glue it onto a similarly round cardboard, punch a hole through the middle and stick a pin through this hole onto a base. Then all you have to do is turn the wheel so fast that for our unaccustomed eye it is seemingly standing still. The only color that you see now is white.

This way you have brought back a cycle of the creation of unity—out of the diversity of the colors the Mandala became again the original white.

The reverse happens in the roses of the Gothic. Not only do they depict the Creation graphically, but the conversion of the light into the multitude of colors lets them become a lasting Creation—in each second the universe is being created anew by the incident light, just as, according to the Hindu belief, the real universe comes into existence anew each moment. When you, while contemplating the rose, suddenly fall through the colorful multitude into the center and all you see is white—in a moment of enlightenment—then the same thing happened that also happened when doing our simple exercise. A cycle of the Creation returned to its beginning. And do not be afraid, it will also begin anew.

In this exercise we want to explain to our intellect, while we are painting, the history of creation of the colors. On the opposite page, leave the inner hexagon of the Star of David white. Now you paint the upper triangle red, the left lower triangle blue and the right lower one yellow, according to the three so-called primary colors.

To make the colors for the triangles in between, follow the arrows and mix the two colors next to each other: i.e., red and yellow result in orange; blue and yellow make green; blue and red become violet. These are the secondary colors. Now you will understand why the color televisions with only three colors can produce all the remaining colors.

You have only to continue to mix each time the two adjacent tips or colors and you will obtain *all* possible color-shades. Examples: Red and orange make red-orange. Yellow and green make yellow-green—and so on without end.

And some more color secrets are revealed by the window-Mandala:
1. The complementary colors are lying opposite each other (as it has to be for the antipodes).
2. Mixed all together, they will result in (grey) white again.
3. Set next to each other, they create the biggest possible contrast.
4. Each complementary color pair contains in it again the three primary colors, which together again produce white.

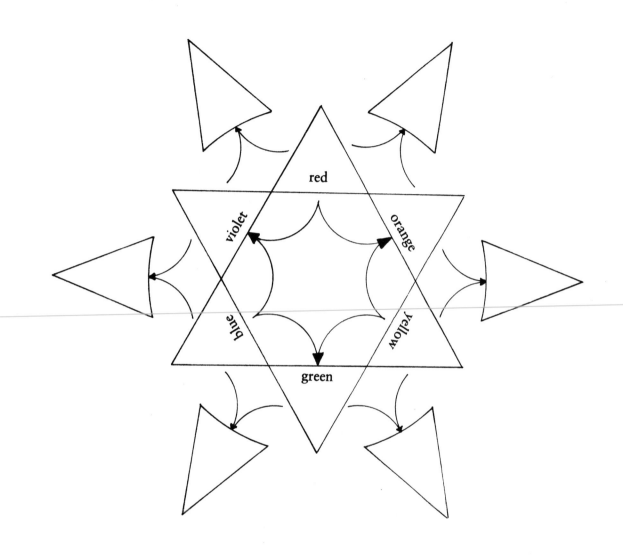

Now another game, one that lets us see colors as an expression of polarity. In a relatively dark room illuminate the following familiar symbol very brightly. Look at it intensely for some minutes. Then close your eyes and observe what appears to your inner eye.

Correct—instead of the black symbol on white ground, now you see a white symbol on black ground: i.e., the complementary. This "after-image" always consists of the opposite or complementary colors! This exercise can show us how close the antipode is to our consciousness. In the truest sense of the word it always lies hidden very close by, in the "shadow." Love and hate lie, as everyone knows, very close to each other—and so each pole has its antipode, each point of view its anti-point-of-view.

Attention: this law has no exception—be aware of it, and it can change your entire life!

An exercise quite a bit beyond the scope of this book would be the following: Whenever you realize that you go too far in one direction, close your eyes for a couple of minutes and during that time collect arguments for the opposite direction. Soon you will realize that the opposite view is equally justifiable, at least from that view. In the end all points of view are equally valid.

The *one* truth, which everybody would like to represent, lies in the center, and it is both as easy and as difficult to see as the pure white light, which has no anti-color anymore, because it is *all* the colors.

The pure light, which has always been a symbol of unity and enlightenment for the esoterics and religion, is not perceptible in the world of polarity. In the Bible it is said that whenever God appears with light-phenomena, human beings are blinded by his brightness. We cannot see God (the unity), and if we come close to him, we cannot bear it. The rose windows became for us meditation and translation of the unity on our level of the polarity. This meditation developed through various stages. Thus the older windows, most distinctly the Romanic arched windows, let the white light fall through the central opening unrefracted, so that the entire light appears in sharp contrast to the darkness in the wall. One of the best examples of this phenomenon is the Creation portrayed in the fifteenth-century cathedral in Astorga, Spain.

In the fully developed roses of the High Gothic, the symbol of the pure white light is then replaced by the symbol of the Logos or of love (Mary).

◆ SYMBOLISM OF COLORS ◆

The predominant colors of Gothic roses are red and blue, the depiction of the polarity of warm and cool. The compromise between these two would be, as we can see in the color-Mandala, violet, which has holy significance in the sacral world of colors (seen, for example, in chasubles, banners, and altar cloths). In the human heart it stimulates spirituality, the path to the center.

Blue symbolizes cold, while at the same time it is the color of the receptive, absorbent, and thus female principle. So it is also the color of the robe of the Virgin Mary, who symbolizes generic female and whose name derives from the blue ocean, *mare*. The ocean symbolizes submersion and descent, and thus the color blue stands for depth, depression, and inertness—as we very well know on a "blue Monday," and when we "feel blue" with a hangover. Blue is the color of the female principle: fertile, propagating.

It signifies other aspects of the creative as well. Vishnu is considered by the Hindus as the Blue God. Hindus also often depict the God of the Search for Truth in blue. Thus blue represents truth, fidelity, and immortality.

As we can sink into the cool blue, *red* lifts us up. It is hot, the color of flames, and thus the color of the Holy Ghost, who came down upon the Disciples in tongues of flame at Whitsuntide (Pentecost). It is the color of courage and of the fire of enthusiasm, and it affects the external world in a similarly stimulating way as the violet affects the internal (world). Furthermore, red stands for passion, and that is why we talk about hot—yes, even burning—love. The Gypsies consider too much red in their caravans as almost precarious, while they always make sure to be surrounded by enough violet as expression of the center.

An important, but understandably rare, color of the rose window is *gold,* which actually belongs only to the "golden center" and mainly served as depiction of the Logos and the sunlight as symbol of the manifested light. In the world of form, gold is reserved for the most significant things. The metal's high material value alone guarantees this. So it is the color and metal of the kings and emperors of the West, but also of all other parts of the world. We have only to think of the legendary gold treasures of the Mayas, Aztecs, and Incas, to whom it was also sacred as the color of their highest goddess, the sun.

Very close to gold is *yellow,* which in its pure form is still considered the color of the light. But as soon as it turns pale or sulfur-colored, it becomes the color of envy, jealousy, betrayal. Judas Iscariot is often depicted in this yellow.

It is also the color of sulfur, that element with which the devil heats up his hell.

The *white,* color of the unrefracted light, as with gold, belongs only to the highest. It is the color of the garments of priests, from the Egyptian priests to Aaron, the first high priest of the Bible, up to the garments of Indian gurus and of the Pope. Besides, it is the color of the Resurrection, and thus it also became the color of the dead, because whoever wants to rise again from the dead has to die in this world—therefore white signifies the resurrection in spirit.

So it is not surprising that in other countries and cultures, as for example in India, it is the color used in funerals. It simply depends on the point of view you hold in regard to dying.

Thus in many countries the flowers of death are white, like those flowers which one gives as a gift there to the resurrected masters. Also the lotus flower, the Eastern symbol of the greatest advancement, is not white by coincidence; it signifies perfection and absolute purity. And now we are back at the beginning, since physical science proves to us (who need proofs for everything) that white is the only perfect color, because it contains all the other colors in itself. White is the universal symbol of purity; we emphasize that in the expressions "snow-white," "swan-white," or "white as a lily."

The other colors are clearly insignificant in the roses, yet you will enjoy using them too when painting the Mandalas. In the American Indian Mandalas, for example, *green* and *brown,* the most common colors of nature, understandably are more common, whereas green as the color of peace can be found often in the roses. Furthermore, we know green as the color of Islam, and as a symbol of growth. Just as the turning green of nature after the long, deathlike (white) winter fills human beings with new hope, so does green symbolize faith and expectation.

Of course there are a lot more associations to the individual colors, and there are also more colors. Take a new look at your already painted Mandalas; think about what your colors may express. Use your intuition to discover more secrets of color.

It is also an interesting exercise to find out what color combinations want to be used: which ones can be found often and which, on the other hand, are rare.

Look closely at *black,* which actually is not a color, because it merely represents the *absence* of all colors, but which nevertheless surrounds all roses, because seen from the inside of the cathedral, the stone structures around the roses seem to be black.

Go back one more time to the symbolism of the white, and the significance of the black will become clear immediately. Just as white portrays everything containing perfection, black is the absolute reduction, the lack of all light and thus of any color.

In astrological symbolism black is the color of Saturn, the Guardian of the Threshold; in our culture it is the color of sorrow and of death. Everybody has to pass through the phase of reduction to the very end; everybody has to pass through the dark pole, the shadow or the underworld, on his/her way to the light.

The roses tell us that symbolically and distinctly, by actually forcing our vision to follow this archetypical course. Coming out of the darkness of the surrounding stone structures, the eye wanders over the colorful periphery of the rose, whose light constantly attracts more light, in order to hold our gaze on the perfect center wherein all is contained.

We have repeatedly found the predominance of red and blue in the cathedral windows. These two colors can be found just as often in the pictures on the tarot cards, in order to express there the same: an aspect of the polar world, the world of contrasts.

A color combination which I have never found in a rose window is red and black. This is also a depiction of polarity, but, as you will probably conclude yourself, of an aspect which does not fit into the image of our churches. After all, these are the colors of the devil, and he officially has no access to Christian churches. Anarchists frequently choose these colors; the Navajo Indians of North America portray their God of Destruction in red and black.

Examining this aspect, it might be worthwhile to have a closer look at national flags. In the German flag, for example, the colors of the devilish black and red are above the gold, the symbol of perfection. The old German trade flag (mercantile) organized the colors of the polarity around the unity in the center: black-white-red.

If you feel like it, sometime you might play with colors and flags and their meanings. It is probably no coincidence that a country like Switzerland—almost the only country in Europe having a peaceful history—also is the only one having a perfect Mandala as a flag. When playing such games, though, it is worthwhile to pay good attention, to avoid being too judgmental.

Here we can learn a lot from "less civilized" cultures; for example, Indians build temples for Shiva, the God of Destruction and Dissolution among their three gods, and they worship him because he is the master of this polar world. Also the Navajos pray to their destructive god described as the Destroyer of Foreign Gods. This god is in charge of all wars and catastrophes of nature. They see him as the bringer of omens, who sends them catastrophes as warnings, in order to lead them back to the right path.

The Kabbalists see in the devil a fallen angel (of which we are still reminded by the last syllable, "el" (in nearly all names of angels), who fell down from a high hierarchy of angels after he had revolted against the Highest Principle. During his fall he pulled our world with him, and it is now the goal of our material existence to climb back up to the light.

We, on the other hand, try to push away into hell the devil, who at one point was to us a Lucifer, a bearer of light. The problem is only that this hell is within us. After all, Christ says it very clearly: his kingdom was not of this world, and the master of this world was precisely this devil. Also the parable of the lost son might lead us to reorganize our values and possibly shed light regarding Lucifer, the bringer of light.

Question: What would the world be without the devil?

Answer: It would not be.[1]

Now, the path led us through the world of colors to the devil, and that is intentional, since, with the exception of white and gold-yellow, the colors also belong in his world. This is because everything that we can see of the most beautiful rose with both inner and outer eyes is part of the polar world, and in this sense devilish.

Very consciously according to this aspect, and with all the understanding that you now have of colors, create the following rose from the Cathedral of León in northern Spain.

---

1. Very illuminating to this topic is the story "Satan," taken from the little book *Chasms of the Heart* by Khalil Gibran. Olten: Walter, 1980.

113

THE EYE MANDALA

The roses have without doubt a certain effect on us, an emanation which radiates from them and communicates with us somehow, comparable perhaps to the effect that is created within a pyramid. Now, I have already introduced the hypothesis that the inner nature of the Mandala has an effect on our inner nature, and those two would recognize each other through their analogous structure. This we want to pursue now more exactly.

It is clear that the theme of the rose, starting with the glass-painting in the center and moving past the colors and forms, including the lead-frames, continues up to the outside stone structures and lets the rose become a harmonic entirety. This harmonic creation affects us directly, starting with our eyes. Consequently we should find a further indication in the eyes. It can be believed that this is actually possible, if we, for example, think of Goethe's sentence "If the eye were not sunlike, the sun could not perceive it."

Now very calmly look at your own eye in the mirror. Then create it in the colors that are most appealing to you.

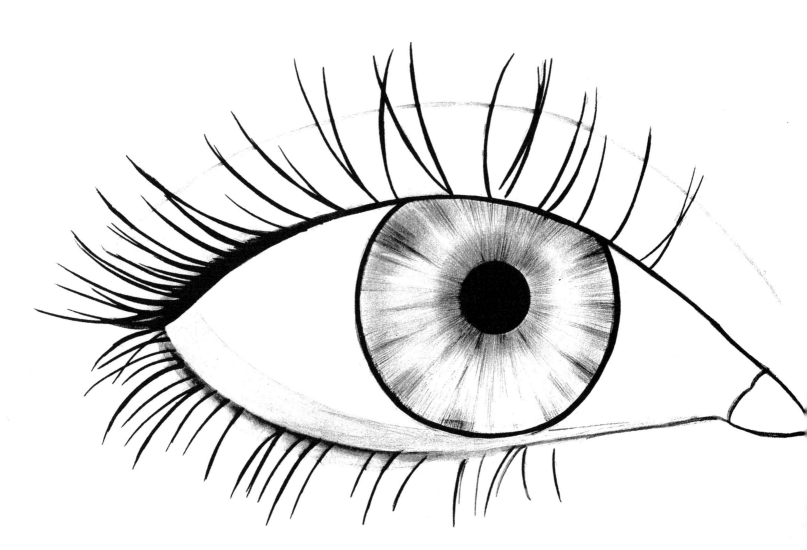

In the New Testament we find at Matthew 6:22 the following saying by Jesus: "The eye is the light of the body. Now if your eye is healthy, then your whole body will be light."

And also this "light of the body" is a Mandala, as you could see in the mirror, and as some of you may know already from studying iridology (see Glossary). One could almost take this sentence from the Gospel of Matthew as a very early basis of iridology, since in fact the eye, and especially the iris, is an image of our organs and literally of the entire human being. Thus, if this, "the mirror of our soul," were completely clear, then we would be totally light, as Jesus told us. In fact, iridology teach us that the more healthfully a human being lives, the more his iris-structure reveals his overall harmony. All deviations from this harmonic structure, like pits or holes, shows a shifting towards the direction of illness (loss of harmony and order).

We never find an ideally structured iris in practice, because the human being in the polar world is ill—after all, he lacks something in order to be whole. Similarly we never find an entirely harmonic horoscope-Mandala. In our polarity, we cannot reach perfection. The best we can do is come very close to it each time. In order to reach the perfection, we have to leave the polarity.

To express this, and not to take upon themselves an attribute that is only for God, the American Indians purposely incorporate small "mistakes" into their sand-Mandalas. Also among the Turkish carpet-weavers one finds this phenomenon of the intentional small "mistake" that they incorporate into their centuries-old patterns, which, by the way, are often very similar to Mandalas.

In our culture, a mistake is by definition something unintentional. But in German, a mistake (Fehler) is something that is missing (fehlen), and thus the Indians and Turkish do justice to the original meaning. They show with their gesture that their creations lack something: the perfection they see only in God. One could imagine in our culture a computer into which, out of humility, one has programmed an intentional mistake!

A carpet dealer from Konja, who had already adapted himself to our Western customs, once told me in resignation that it was simply impossible to knock out of these simple people the nonsense of the intentional mistake, since otherwise they feared the evil eye. But with the evil eye the carpet-weavers mean God's wrath, and it is their understanding (as with the one of the American Indians) that God or the Great Spirit sees everything that happens here on earth, so that all tricks and deceptions are senseless right from the beginning. So they leave the perfection up to God.

Technically, the windows of the Gothic are not absolutely correctly executed. Their harmony obviously depends on other laws, laws which our eye—whether we experience that consciously or not—recognizes instinctively. In the Mandala of the eye there is only one possibility for perfect harmony: something divine. Today it is possible, with the help of complicated electronic devices, to tune musical instruments to technically absolute pitch—only then they do not sound beautiful. In order to convey harmony, the instrument has to be tuned by a human being, even when, or probably because, he has faults.

But let us come back to the sense of sight. It is not only the Turkish women who think of God as the All-Seeing Eye. Even in Western culture God is often symbolized by an eye. Usually this eye is shaped like a triangle or it is round. Still today the simple, round window of the early churches is called "oculus" (=Latin for "eye").

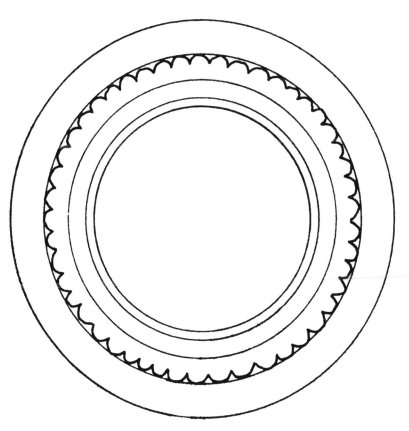

Our visible eye consists of the white, the multicolored iris with its many structures, and the black pupil in the center. Optically this black spot is only being created by the fact that there is actually nothing, a hole. All light is being swallowed here and steered inside to the retina. This way the rose is comparable to the eye: the white, completely impervious to light, corresponds with the external stone structures, the colorful iris with the colored glass-elements, and the pupil with the center of the rose, through which the vision is supposed to glide into the reality of the Logos behind it. The center-point of each Mandala is the Nothing, the emptiness, and thus the *Unity* and the *Entirety*—here nothing and everything exists in potential.

The inner eye (retina) only repeats this Mandala structure. From the periphery to the inside the vision-cells become closer and closer to each other so that the vision becomes clearer and clearer the closer to the center—then directly in the middle there is the "blind spot," where nothing can be seen, and all the information is being channelled by the optic nerve backwards to the brain.

By the way, the eye is a direct part of the brain, that is, the physical brain. Earlier we were introduced to the Mandala-structure of the brain. So it is the same process with each Mandala: the periphery gathers the vision and moves it through the center onto a new level which is located behind it (compare again the action of a burning-glass). Through the center it is possible to leave the two-dimensional surface and to get into the third dimension of the space located behind it; and under certain circumstances it is even possible to fall into a fourth dimension which is located further behind the third.

While painting the retina-picture, experience this principle which leads into the depth.

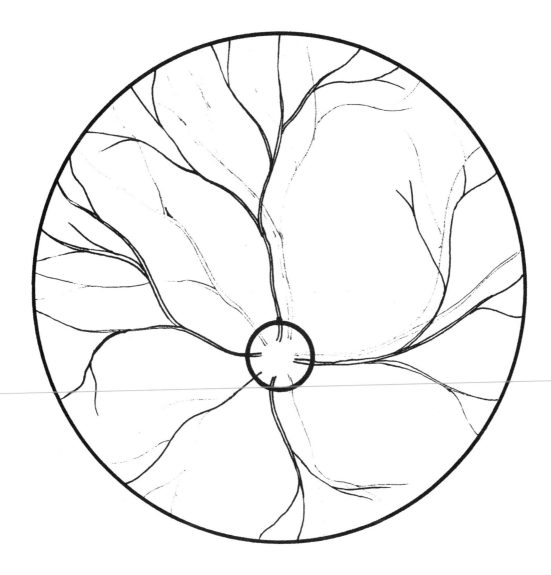

Without sun there is no light, no vision, no recognition. The eye is our mediator between the external light of the sun and the internal light of the recognition. And this internal light corresponds with the external one—as outside so inside—just as each light on earth corresponds with the light of the sun—as above so below.

The Mandala of the eye shows us the connection between the original Mandala of the sun and the original Mandala of the inner vision that we symbolically portray as the third eye, as the shining heart of Jesus, as rose or as chakra.

When we learn to see Mandalas in the outside, in the world of the polarity, our inner self learns from that to discover its true nature. If we make ourselves aware that everything in the outside only mirrors our inner self, then in the Mandala we experience our true Being. This means one can recognize in *each* Mandala one's true Being—the center recognizes the center—only the Being can discover the Being.

Thus, the eye shows us many things, when we look behind its façade and when we advance from the external eye to the internal vision. Mostly we depend too much on appearances, although those will always deceive us.

◆ THE WORLD OF FORMS ◆

After our eyes have seen through the world of the colors, we will turn to the forms and structures. Just as all colors flow out of the one white light, so do all forms grow out of the one point, which, as we have said, does not even exist as form. This point, as original point, gives birth to all forms and structures. Following the form-structure of the rose, we will reach the point again and again, the same way that the colors again and again lead us to the white of the center. As we found certain laws behind the colors in the polar world, so do such laws lie behind the forms: the laws of geometry, the laws of numbers. All Mandalas, especially the rose windows, are constructed according to certain relations of numbers, as you probably have already realized. Everywhere we meet 4, 6, 8, 12, and 24 elements. Also the number of the center, of the unity, should be clear: 1 (the one).

◆ THE WORLD OF NUMBERS ◆

If wheel and rose are models of the universe, we have to find behind them the same numbers and relations as behind the Creation. Let us have a look first at the numbers and their meaning:

The **1** correlates with the unity, the not yet manifested, the highest: God.

The **2** is obviously the number of polarity, of contrasts, thus of this world (and thus of the devil).

The **3**, on the other hand, expresses again a harmonic aspect of the Creation, a divine one, but in contrast to the 1, the 3 is a level which is already revealed. Thus we talk about the Holy Trinity (Father, Son, and Holy Ghost), and the Three Wise Men; but also the Hindus know this trinity in their three gods: Brahma, Vishnu, and Shiva—analogous to the three Gunas (the vital life forces of this creation).

These correlate again exactly with the three basic vectors which (in the opinion of our scientists) build up the world of forces and of effects. Also the three primary colors symbolize this correlation, just as white, of course, correlates with the One. In the triangle we see geometrically how the 3 grew beyond the 2.

The **4** is the number of the cross with its four extreme points, the four directions, constructed with the two beams of the polarity. The cross and the square are symbols of substance and thus of our world. It is this cross that we have to take upon us. It is also the cross that Christ took upon him, when he came out of the unity (1) into the world (4) and in this way united both; that's why Christ's number then is the 5.

Also in the world of numbers do we find again symbolism known to us. From the one center-point the cross is being stretched in four directions and it forms the world. In this center-point the four directions disappear again, and also the two beams of the polarity again become the one in their crossing-point. So, of course, the world has also four elements (fire, water, air, and earth); the fifth element of the Hindus, Akasha (the point), does not belong to the material world. So there are four world-rivers, four kinds of roots, four seasons, and four world-eras.

The **5** is the number of the human being, as the pentagonal star of the Mandala of the human being shows us, and it is also the number of Christ on the cross in his human aspect with his five wounds. The five-pointed star, surrounded by stone, results in the pointed arch of the Gothic.

The **6** is a different symbol of the polarity on an even further developed level. Think of the two triangles of the Star of David, the one red and the other blue, penetrating each other, portraying the penetration of the micro- and macrocosm. With this level correlate our six rainbow colors and man and woman as directly opposite beings and thus also "sex" as the expression of the world of human beings that is reproducing itself.

The **6** also stands for the equilibrium between the forces, which we can see in the six-pointed star.

In the **7** we meet again a number that is related to harmony. It stands for the Entirety on an already clearly material level—thus God wrought the entire Creation in seven days. There are seven classical planets, the seven liberal arts, seven virtues (frequent themes of the roses), and seven periods of life. The ancients considered the 7 a mystical number.

In general we can see that the uneven numbers continue the direct development of the 1, whereas the even numbers remain more connected with the 2 and thus with the polarity. Thus, the series of numbers traces the path from one extreme to the other, from the pole to the antipode, similar to the way that in the zodiac a positive sign always alternates with a negative one.

To this effect the **8** continues the development of the 4. Through the world of the foursome, with its four directions and four paradise-rivers, blow the eight world-winds (which are still being used in our meteorology of today). The **8**, in its form as lying-down lemniscate, stands for infinity and thus is also symbol of the rebirth. It is not a coincidence that the lemniscate in esoterics (e.g., above the head of the magician of the first tarot card) and in mathematics are used in the same sense.

The **9** concludes this first cycle of the numbers, symbolizing fruition, perfection, universality. It points to a time for withdrawal and introspection, a time for rounding out.

With the **10** a new chapter begins. The 10 corresponds in the symbolism of the numbers with the 1 and the initial point. Purely graphically, the 10 is a 1 with a 0. And in this 0 we can see the point again, that original point which is blown up by space and so corresponds with the 1, the unmanifested.

The new beginning with the 10 is also illuminated by another point of view. The esoteric views the numbers according to their symbolic value, and adds up the compound numbers until they become one figure again (so-called Theosophical Addition). According to this, 10 $(1+0) = 1$; 11 $(1+1) = 2$; 12 $(1+2) = 3$; 13 $(1+3) = 4$; so that, as you can see now, the cycle in fact starts all over again. So, for example, is the 18 $(1+8) = 9$, and the 40 becomes 4 again. The 52 weeks of the year are reduced to 7, the number of days in the week. And the 12 Apostles express the three-in-one God on a material level. The 12 has still another independent significance—i.e., perfection—if we think of Israel's 12 tribes, the 12 signs of the zodiac, and the 12 months of the year.

Thus, if a rose is constructed according to the scheme 6-12 ($\hat{=}3$) or 24 ($\hat{=}6$) or 48 ($\hat{=}3$), we see that there is always the same idea behind it. Often in the roses, but particularly in the Indian and Tibetan Mandalas, the number systems 3 and 4 are combined with the rows that lie directly behind them. We remember the 4, the square, as expression of the material world, and the 3, the trinity (triangle), as emanation of the divine (compare, for example, the Divine Eye as triangle). These two levels united in one symbol result in the mystical number 7.

One could criticize that there are so many similar meanings for different numbers (e.g., 3, 5, 7, 9) and ask why there are so many symbols in order just to express the same thing. One can point out that the different systems each have different emphases and they, in their diversity, are most likely to do justice to the complexity of the Creation.[1]

Let us make it clear that no one system is better than another one, and that argument about systems is totally senseless. One can express the same truth in the system of 2 of Yin-Yang; or in the system of 3 of the Gunas or of the primary colors; or in the system of 4 of the elements and the seasons; or in the fivefold of the Chinese doctrine of elements (which in turn is based on the system of 2 of the Yin and Yang); or in the system of 10 of Arabic numbers; or in the system of 12 of astrology and time; or in the system of 22 of the Kabbalah; and on and on. They all fulfill their purpose, each in its place, they supplement one another and they never exclude one another.

An astrologer who thinks the *I Ching* is pointless has neither understood its essence nor the essence of astrology.

If, on the other hand, one perceives the claim to express the Entirety with so few symbols as impossible or too speculative, one might at least recognize the parallels existing in the present time—our time that is so unreceptive to mysticism. There all our computers work according to the system of 2 (binary system), which is exactly in accordance with the Chinese Yin-Yang, expressed in the T'ai Chi symbol. Also our major mathematical systems, which seem to us to be almost omniscient, in the end can only distinguish between plus and minus, between yes and no—but they can certainly do that very fast. All color television systems work according to a system of 3 and thus produce the entire spectrum of colors.

Most impressive, perhaps, is the relationship between the genetic code of DNA and the *I Ching*. Just as the genetic code works with four signs (the acids), which it combines in a system of 3 (codon) and which thus has 64 "letters," so is the *I Ching* made of two signs, which are arranged each in systems of 3 and this also results in 64 "letters" (hexagrams). The genetic code is completely universal; the albumin of each human being, animal, or plant is created according to the coherent system of encoding. Thus the DNA forms the basis of all life on the biological level. Why then shouldn't the *I Ching* symbolize the entire life on the psychological level?

Now fill in this rose with colors—and at the same time pay attention to the symbolism of numbers hidden in it.

---

1. You will find a parallel to this in biology, where the genetic code (which determines the entire diversity of the organic life) is provided with far more possibilities of expression than necessary.

With this rose (it is the north-rose of Chartres) you now have painted all three roses of this unique Gothic cathedral. The two others are on pages 95 and 109. Have a look at all three together one more time. All three were constructed according to the 12-key, and they become, from the standpoint of geometry, more and more similar toward the center. Only toward the outside, the periphery, does each stress another aspect of the Creation.

Behind the manifest geometry there is in most of the roses another, deeper, subtle level of order; and behind everything is finally the symbolic level. Thus also geometry (which Pythagoras says was divine, because of the timeless constancy of the harmony of numbers which is concealed in it) serves the same goal as already light and color do. Geometry is also expression of the longing for the infinite in a finite world. This becomes even more evident in the sacral art of Islam, because here the geometry becomes, by entirely avoiding figurative elements, an even more direct approach to the search for God.

To the dervishes, whom one could call the mystics of Islam, the perimeter of a circle means the law (of the globe); the radius means the path; and the center, the point, means truth.

Thus we have a complete conformity with the Christian version of the roses. In the perimeter of the circle we find physical life with its laws: e.g., the law of polarity, expressed in the opposition of vice and virtue, or in the zodiac. All radii (paths) here lead to the center, wherein is the Logos, which also for us represents truth.

On the opposite page you see an Islamic Mandala.

123

✦ THE HEALING OF ROSES ✦

Christ says of himself: "I am the way, the truth and the life." All in one. Whether or not we know about the lawful order, our eye absorbs the inner harmony of the symbolic geometry and positions it in relation to our internal patterns. Nobody will experience chaotic feelings and perceptions while gazing on the Gothic roses. They do not evoke chaos in us, because they do not have a resonance for that. Instead they connect us, through their internal and external order, with the cosmos of the internal order in us. In case you should experience conflicting emotions while painting these roses, then this is not due to the roses, but to your still prevailing incapability of experiencing their harmony; or it is due to something inside you that offers resistance to this harmony.

The contemplation of these timeless symbols is psychotherapy in its truest and deepest function—confrontation of the human being in all his depth—because behind all chaos in us also lies the cosmos. Certainly it is our task, not to suppress but to confront the chaos; but the path has to lead through it to the order (cosmos), and it is therefore important not to lose sight of the goal. Actually, it is impossible to lose it, because of the inner balance of the universe.

Thus we saw the roses, which show us this path, come into existence just at a time when the darkness of this world was at its deepest and the path seemed almost to be lost. Possibly we live in a similar time today, since in the external materialism, the internal sparks threaten to suffocate. However we do it, we carry in ourselves the entire development of mankind; and thus in each of us the Inquisition is still alive, with its projection of guilt onto the outside (today the heretics and witches are just called differently).

But in every one of us there still exists the experience of unity, the condition of Paradise. All in one. This memory is recalled by the Mandalas, which, after all, symbolize everything in one and the One in everything. Preoccupation and experience with them can give us the strength to confront and accept the antipode, the chaos. It probably happened this way eight hundred years ago, when the people who created the cathedrals and roses gained from this activity the strength to find their path despite all the distractions. We have a modern parallel to this old experience just behind us. During the time of chaos of the Nazi regime with its system of modern inquisition, denunciation, and persecution, the Christian church gained there, where it was still alive, an entirely new strength and energy—which, in the years since the Nazi threat was overcome, increasingly deteriorates again! Like all contrasts, chaos and cosmos lie close to each other, and we can grow through either of them.

And we grow especially then, when we ourselves are deeply involved, when we become targets, or when we let ourselves be touched. What we said about the builders of the cathedrals and roses holds similarly true for us. There, where we are immersed in the task, something can happen with us, something can start to move. That can also occur while we are reading, but much more likely it will happen while we are meditating or painting. . . . The emotions that arise do not always have to be nice or pleasant, although they often are—but sometimes unwillingness, anger, and impatience arise while we are painting.

How can that be? Well, the Mandala contains everything, and so, in principle, it can also extract everything from us. So sometimes we might not succeed immediately in uniting the conflicts in our center in harmony again. We will especially realize this when we do the Mandala games.

What is there to do?

Nothing. As always, just *observe* what is going on—sooner or later the penny will drop and you will realize that it cannot be the Mandala's fault, that it is perfect in itself, and you will go and get the colored pencil out of the corner. In the outside nothing is ever guilty, it can always only be we who are guilty!

Attention: This sentence is dangerous, if you really let it get to you—dangerous for all your viewpoints, prejudices, and positions.

Now construct your own fantasy-Mandala on the emptiness of the next page. Let yourself get inspired by everything that you have heard about forms, colors, and geometry. There cannot be any copying or imitating. In other words, whatever you do is an imitation of the Creation. Therefore take courage!

In the truest sense of the word there are innumerable, unlimited Mandala variations. One danger of this book lies in having to restrict oneself on account of the patterns. Yet they should stimulate and inspire you to find the path to your *own* Mandalas—inner and outer. . . . Find (in the sense of becoming open-minded and attentive to) the Mandalas which surround us on the outside. Wake up to the Mandalas which live inside of us. Whenever the patterns are not perfect, that may not be intended, but it is good, because in their limitation lies a chance to outgrow the barriers and limits.

Now you need a simple compass, a ruler, and a pencil, and then you begin. And begin there, where everything begins—in the center!

Make sure that your Mandala remains symmetrical. You will succeed in doing this by letting it grow layer by layer in concentrical circles evenly from the inside to the outside. Once you have finished constructing it, color it.

✦ FANTASY MANDALA ✦

◆ MEDITATION ◆

Now contemplate your own work and let it have a retroactive effect on you: give it back to your consciousness out of which it has just grown; look at it without judging it, without recognizing details; instead experience the whole, the undivided. This pattern of order, which in all its aspects has to be a projection, a creation of your inner being, you fetch back, you let it come inside again—just as Brahma inhales and exhales his creation. You then close the circle.

During such a process you may experience the symbolic structures of the Mandala—which are, after all, images of you, including your own corporeality—and you may feel its individual parts in your respective organs and body parts. Resonance is a vibration phenomenon, and the Mandala is our own vibration-circle, which retroactively can cause us to vibrate. Let yourself be incorporated in the vibrations!

On the opposite page you find a very simple Mandala, a circle, which you can fill with all the chaos that is in yourself. Paint into it all of yourself that has finally had enough of the constant talk about harmony, unity, etc.: that is, your dark side, which exists whether you want to admit this or not. Give your dark side a place in your book as well as your light side.

If you do not want to do this, the world will keep on turning. Your shadow will then look for its own space in little mistakes or in fits of anger in your Mandala Book— and in your Mandala, where the shadow is missing.

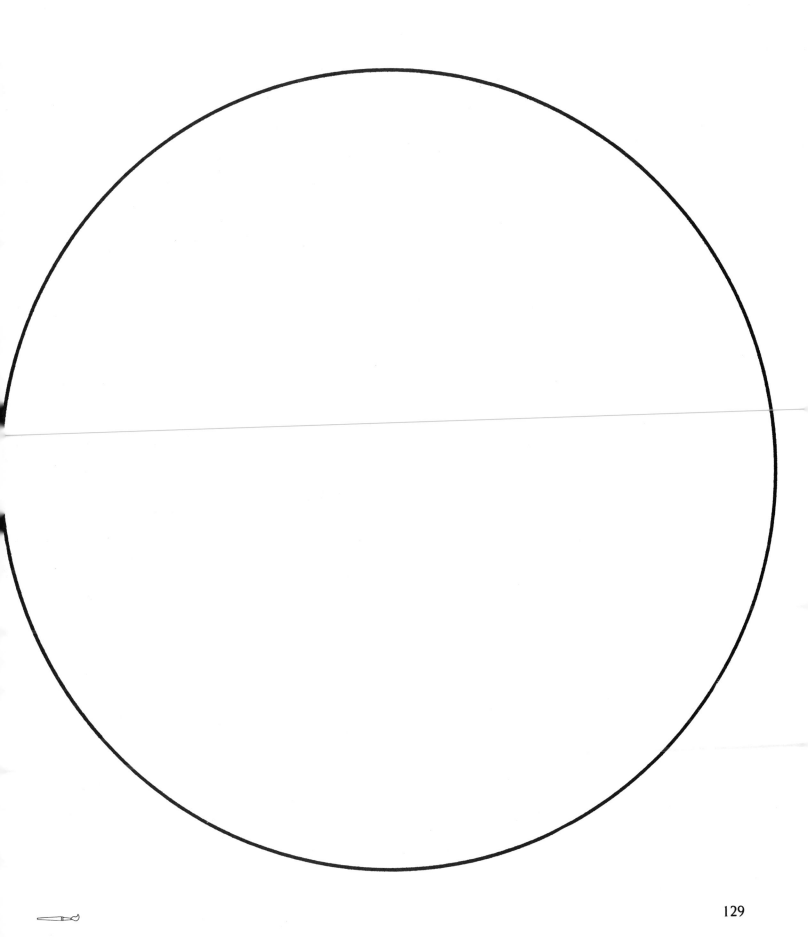

All the knowledge about light and shadow, colors, forms, and the order of numbers was available to the architects of the Gothic, and they used it in their rose windows, in order to express the One and the All. They partially copied the basic geometric concept from the original images of nature. In the Cathedral of Lyon, for example, we find in the rose of a small side chapel a portrayal of the Creation in the form of an original whirl, which may depict a spiral nebula as well as a cyclone or a whirlpool—but also that whirl with which we enter this world and with which we leave it again: the already well-known principle of the calm at the center of the storm.

With your colors, try to come close to the dynamics of this rose. The original is created in the contrasting colors of warmth (red) and coldness (blue).

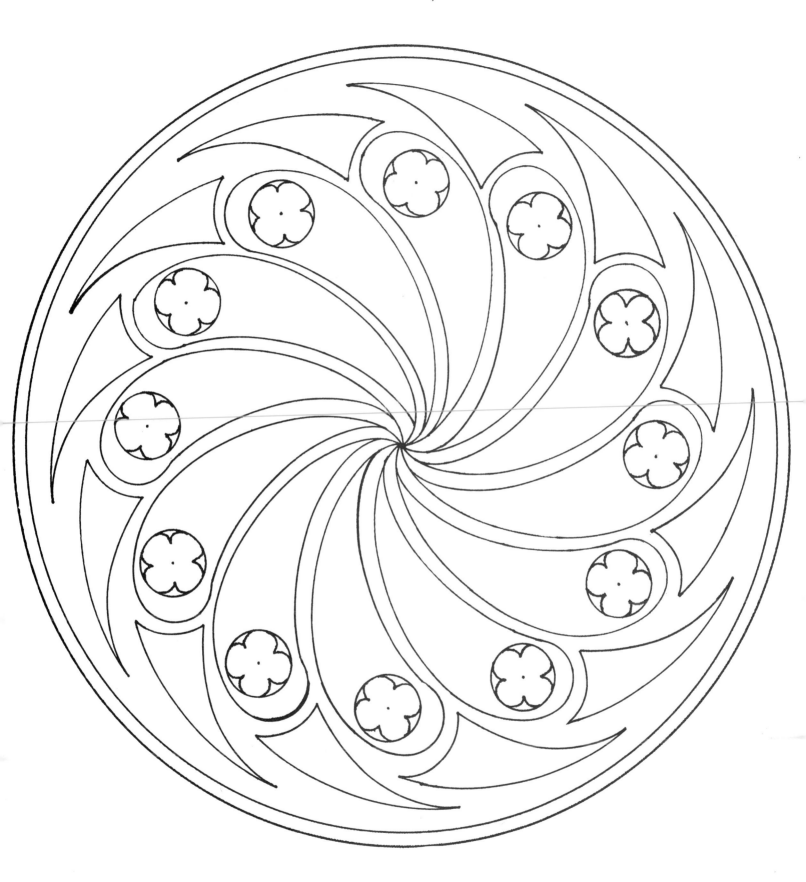

The north-rose of Sées reveals to us the secret of snow-flakes, those uncounted Mandalas of the winter. The rose is created exactly according to their principle. All snow-flakes are six-pointed stars having the strictest symmetry, and they are all different. In symbolism, the six-pointed star signifies the unification and interpenetration of the divine and the earthly worlds.

Even with no further proof, this phenomenon of the snowflake should be sufficient to make it clear once and forever that there are unlimited shapes of the One (Mandala).

133

The development of the rose windows throughout time leads us finally to the flame-roses of the late Gothic, which, in combination of structure, color, and light, evoke the impression of fire, and often supposed to depict the flame-tongues of the Holy Ghost.

Now create such a flame-rose with the appropriate colors into a real fireball. The basic structure corresponds with the rose of Amiens, which, by the way, around its periphery still contains the symbolism of the wheel of fortune.

135

✦ THE ROSE ✦

Now we want to have a look at the symbol of the rose that gave the windows of the cathedrals its name. In Western tradition a special meaning is accorded to the rose among all flowers, comparable to the lotus blossom of the East. The thousand-petaled lotus, which blooms on the head of the illuminated, has its parallel in the halo, the nimbus, the aureole of Christian saints' images.

What does the symbol of the rose tell us? In the religious art of that time, we notice its relation to the Virgin Mary, who is often portrayed with roses, sometimes in a rose garden, and to whom also the rosary, that ritualized prayer characterized by its constant repetitions, is dedicated. And this rosary in turn takes us back to the East, because it probably corresponds with the Hindu Mala, which from there came to the Arabs and then, brought along by the Knights of the Cross, became the rosary in our culture. The rosary prayer in its monotony resembles the heart prayer of the Church of the East, and even the mantrams of the Tibetan prayer wheels—yes, it even has a certain resemblance to the Koan of Zen.

All these rituals aim at eliminating the intellect through fatigue, and in this way arrive at existential God-experiences. Thus the Hail Mary, said over and over, provides a link among cultures. The Christians—as well as the Islamic Sufis—consider Mary as exemplifying the love that opens itself up and sacrifices itself, the symbol of which, in turn, has always been the rose, as the flower of Isis, Aphrodite, Venus, and Mary. Thus the rose windows are also windows of love; and often Mary, personification of love, is standing in the center, the symbol of the One.

At this point it is worthwhile mentioning that Dante, in his *Divine Comedy,* gives Paradise the shape of the rose. Paradise, in turn, is the place of unity, of the nonseparation from God.

As sign of love the rose is also symbol of acceptance, one of the meanings of love. And this way it also becomes a symbol of suffering. To the mysticism of the thirteenth century, love was a synonym for the union with God (compare also the medieval German love poetry of that time and the love poems of the Sufis—e.g., those by Rumi). To the alchemists the rose was the "flower of the knowing," and they talked about a "rosarium philosophorum," a philosophical rose garden. The north-rose of Paris, you may remember, is called the alchemist's rose.

Letting the rose windows affect us totally, we find another analogy to the rosary in the monotony of the forms and ornaments, which are also tiring for the mind, and are therefore suited to free the spirit for a moment from the limits of space and time.

Last but not least are the largest and most beautiful cathedrals, the "Notre Dame" churches, dedicated to the Virgin Mary. L. Charpentier writes in his book *The Secret of the Cathedral of Chartres* that these Notre Dame churches of France are located on sites which, looked at from a great height, resemble the star image of the Virgin—another secret of the Gothic.

Possibly under the symbol of Mary, at the prime of the Gothic, there was an attempt between East and West to open up and to reconcile. The Order of the Knights Templar, to which we owe the rosary and which adopted the symbol of Mary, had become at that time the richest and most influential organization besides the papacy and the kingdom of France. Despite their task of fighting Islam, the Templars had obviously begun to open up to the wisdom-teachings of the East and to come to an understanding with the "Three Wise Men from the East." Either through that, or even before, a core of this order had developed into an esoteric Christianity. Many facts support such a presumption, among others the finally unsolved end of the order and the mysterious events when it was dissolved, up to the attempt of the papacy to completely erase its traces.

Possibly there is also a connection to the Cathars, those Manichaean-oriented "heretics" who, for their ideal of the pure, spiritual love, were burned at the stake in thousands during the Inquisition. The Templars had openly refused to participate in the crusade against the Cathars.

The rose cross, which always had a connection with the esoteric beliefs, is a Manichaeic symbol; in a Mandala it unites the signs of the physical world and ultramundane love (4 + 1).

Paint this rose window to show the harmony and love between the polar forces.

THE JOURNEY
THROUGH THE LABYRINTH

All that we experienced in the roses, we could have similarly discovered in other forms of expression of the Mandala. One of these forms is the labyrinth, which has tight connections to the Gothic and its cathedrals. Thus, labyrinths exist today, even though covered up, in the cathedrals of Amiens, Bayeux, Poitiers, Saint-Quentin. In other cathedrals—Reims, Sens, Arras, Auxerre—the labyrinths of later times were destroyed also. The journey through the world of roses corresponds with the one through the world of the labyrinths. The same destination awaits us.

Labyrinths are just as difficult to place in time as the Mandala itself. We find them in Megalithic epochs, as on a stone near Pontevedra, Spain. They appeared in many countries during the same time period. There are Celtic and Minoan, Etruscan and Babylonian versions. We find them in classical Rome and Greece, and in a spiral form in Sweden's Gotland, in New Zealand, in northern Germany, and in England—yes, even in Vietnam. In the Middle Ages, in the cathedrals of France and Italy there was often a labyrinth.

In the Cathedral of Chartres, probably the most secretive and most important of all cathedrals, the best-known labyrinth is preserved. Until very recently the Bishop of Chartres supposedly staged dances on it. Here the two symbols of the path, along which the soul has to go throughout life, are combined to make a single symbol. The rose of the west portal, which portrays the Last Judgment, with the division of souls between heaven and hell, corresponds exactly in space and dimension with the labyrinth on the ground of the cathedral. Also this labyrinth has the form of a Mandala, and like each labyrinth it symbolizes the search of the human being, the search which—along the most varying paths, sometimes closer to the center, then again further away—finally leads to the *one* center. In old days the faithful imitated this path symbolically, by following the course of the labyrinth into the center, as penitence or ritualized pilgrimage while, for example, they were sliding on their knees.

In this center, in the Cathedral of Chartres, they were greeted by a six-petaled white marble-rose, which is exactly congruent with the rosette in the center of the west-portal-rose, when one imagines the wall folded down onto the floor. Obviously those two Mandalas of the same size correspond with each other, and projecting them in thought one on top of the other, we will receive the doctrine twice: There is *one* path, and it leads along numerous deceptive detours to the *one* center. Here the dangers of this path are indicated as well, because just as one can get lost in despair in the labyrinth (i.e., get stuck in the polarity), on the journey one could also stumble over the edge through the periphery of the rose between heaven and hell, between good and evil. Once one has encountered and overcome all these dangers, one may expect to encounter the Logos, to enter the heart of the rose as symbol of completion and love.

With the following exercise we want to connect two paths, the one of the labyrinth of Chartres with the one of the light. The goal of this exercise is to follow the path of the labyrinth with the colors, starting with black in the outer border until finally in the center of the rose you reach white. In most of the roses you will find your way home to the light, travelling the brilliantly colored path empty of spirit into the white, the wholeness and abundance.

You will find this same idea on the cover of this book; if necessary, you can use those colors to orient yourself.

• MEDITATION OF THE POINTS •

Now contemplate your own work and imagine yourself becoming smaller and smaller, until finally you are a small, black point, the right size to fit through the narrow alleys of the labyrinth that you just painted and that is now in front of you. Throughout this meditation, you and this primary point are one and the same. You, this point, swim more or less aimlessly through the blackness of the space outside the labyrinth—seeking and not knowing what— and then the point comes across something lighter, dark blue. Now it knows what it is looking for: light. So it tries to proceed further. Again and again it finds small entrances, but they all lead to the same dark barrier which separates it from the light. Thus it tries in vain to penetrate, and much time elapses, while it goes around in circles. It fights and rages and deliberates, often changing direction, but nothing helps.

Finally, when it stops resisting, accepts the border, and only aimlessly follows it, it suddenly stumbles into an entrance after all—and immediately gets its hopes up again and proceeds directly towards the goal. It even realizes how it is beginning to absorb the light; now the point becomes lighter and lighter, soon lighter than the others, entirely dark blue—and that is when it loses its direct way again—stagnation. It does not get farther away, although it does not come any closer—and then it suddenly finds the right direction, and again it approaches straight on—and finds itself on the wrong path—again stagnation. And then it happens, it—you—the small point marches directly into the goal, into the center—and nevertheless does not reach it. There remains still a thin wall between it and the light, and it tries with all its powers, goes on moving, and then this path even wants to lead it away again, into the dark, but it does not go along, not it, this most brilliant of all blue points, it does not go into the dark anymore. . . . Something has to be wrong with the path.

The point now invents a system for itself; many plausible arguments all confirm that the point—you—is right and that the path (therefore the whole) needs urgently to be corrected, improved, or fundamentally reformed. But as much as it may achieve and as hard as it tries, the world does not really get any better through that system. At the beginning the point felt quite optimistic, but it in the course of time the entire system proved to be like Sisyphus rolling his boulder uphill only to see it roll down again—so the doubts become more and more oppressive and finally lead the point to terrible desperation.

Then, an enormous breakthrough!—along comes another point. Of course the first one ignores it, because this one is not quite as blue as itself—still rather dirty-blue. This vagrant point actually goes around the curve—and that serves it right—back into the darkness! And then it again passes the first point. The first point follows the second—clandestinely, of course—on the side of the light. The other one inevitably will go astray—there are innumerable precedents for that. But this is strange—although the other one made clear mistakes and directly moved into the dark, it does not therefore become dark again. Yes, one could almost say the intruder becomes somewhat lighter— maybe a little bit violet. Now, of course, the first point would be the last one to consider violet a nice color. After some cogitation it even finds arguments that clearly speak against violet, arguments that practically deny that it is a color. And then this crazy vagrant point, this intruder, simply disappears around the next curve toward the darkness, and the world is back in order.

When other points come along and suffer the same fate, the original point is already prepared, warns of the violet danger and can even save some from taking the wrong way—they then become its grateful supporters. Thus it actually becomes a prophet of the terrible violet and it grows old in honors. The only thing that interferes with its system a bit is the fact that one does not hear anything anymore from the violet points. The vagrant one (which a long time ago turned totally orange and which some of the first point's own supporters then followed)—this one it could soon expose as being a plump seducer and envier of its own fame. But the orange color of this point once in a while makes the blue point think, and sometimes it gets doubts about its own system, and then it has a vague memory that even it was once searching for something such as light and that this orange possibly has something to do with that.

But what does it matter? It is old and deep blue, the facts speak a distinct language. Its system of the blue pointology was developed and confirmed in its lifetime by the blue points—especially by the researchers among them, up to the blue axiom of the blue planet and to the violet parable of repulsion.

Then all of a sudden something happens that actually cannot happen. There, where innumerable research studies have proved no point can ever get to—in that brilliant white behind the border—there appears . . . a point. One cannot determine the color of this point—one can barely perceive it, that's how blinding it is over there—but what it says over the wall affects the old point. Puzzled yet confident, very quietly and calmly it sets off around the corner, which until now was the end of the world, into the dark. And many colors come along with it, and none says anything. They are even already turning a bit violet.

And again it comes to the curve where the path continues into darkness—and it and most of them go farther. A few refuse here, in fear of even more darkness. The old point goes on, and again around in a circle and another curve, and even farther away from the light; and again some stay behind, and it goes on, in a new circle, this time in another direction, rounds another curve into the dark, and this time nearly all stay behind—but the old point still remembers the voice from the white, whispering over the wall, and goes on changing direction, circling again, far beyond where it has gone before, until finally the path leads back to the light, and the young points, its former supporters, overtake it and flow ahead—to the light.

The next curve leads to the light, and also the next, and the next after the next, and it becomes strangely reddish, a completely new color, of which one had never heard in the history books of the points. Only in completely unbelievable tales told by visionaries and story-tellers had one heard of something like that—and now it itself had come upon this strangely reddish color. But what was left now to frighten it, after all the disappointments of its long life?

Finally it is standing again opposite the light—only this time one sees it from the other side—and the point has become rather red itself, and some of its old pupils have already researched everything, have explored the borders of the new world and discovered that it really does not go forward anymore—the road ahead leads straight back into the dark.

The old truth, nevertheless, had now been confirmed by the fact that one could not reach the white—although the solution, of course, lay in the red, and red was a historic error and a backward step. One wanted to send messengers back regularly, who were supposed to free all points from the blue and violet level. In case that did not help, one might even resort to violence—in the name of the red pointology.

The old point takes delight in the light, and it does not say anything, does not contradict, and when it nevertheless and without any sensation continues around the curve into renewed darkness, it does not persuade anybody to come along, because it has discovered that it itself knows little about what will come up. Nevertheless, when another point follows on its own initiative, the old point is pleased and tells it about its presentiments and also that story about the orange point, which had appeared a long time ago and had started up strange rumors. Then a legend about yellow points, which supposedly had existed unconceivably long ago, comes to its mind.

And the road is infinitely long and winding and leads farther and farther into the dark. They become gradually redder and redder, and when they themselves even turn orange, they are not surprised about anything anymore.

They now face the absolute darkness, and that is the most terrifying of all. There are many situations in which the one needs the help of the other. What supports them most is the new hope—which they do not pass on, though, because after all that, who can still be sure?—the hope, namely, that the direct path is a winding one, that one's own color becomes lighter the farther one proceeds. Many things, in turn, confirm this intuition, but from all their life experiences and from the old legends and fairy tales, which they now believe implicitly, they have learned to be careful.

Then on their long circular paths, they also become certain that they need even the darkness, in order to become lighter themselves. Yes, the world soon seems to them merely paradox: the more darkness they let in, the lighter they themselves become. And then also that becomes more and more certain, and out of the resistance to the darkness there develops a humble and grateful path which leads *through* it—who would have ever thought so? They feel gratitude for the dark, they cannot understand anymore what is happening, and they have already stopped thinking about it—that's how deeply the two have already thought.

They now both believe in also becoming yellow, and when it happens, it is simple and okay. And finally this yellow becomes brighter, and the path leaves the dark and leads into the light (and when it deviates once again, this is just as okay). They continue to go on because they go; actually all reasoning has long stopped. And then they see the shining bright goal—and the one approaches it and enters and becomes the white light, and the other one turns back to the colorful points, and their decisions are equally important.

In the labyrinth
Of the clear signs
Losing
To find
Everything
In order to lose
Everything
Nothing

Originally, in the center of the rose of the labyrinth of Chartres, there was a panel with a bull's head—a clear sign of the Minoan labyrinth. Behind the symbolism of that, which at first sight seems contradictory, there is the same idea, only the path here is reversed. Here in the center the monster is lurking, the Minotaur, and the Redemption lies in the outside. The hero in this case has to go into the labyrinth (life); there he has to defeat the monster (the devil, the polarity); and with the help of the famous thread of Ariadne he, now redeemed, finds his way out again.

With or without bull's head, the symbolism remains clear-cut. Everywhere we find different signs, behind which the same things are concealed. In literature, in Homer's *Odyssey*, the hero has to fight his way back to his homeland through a true labyrinth of difficulties. The same applies to Dante's *Divine Comedy* and to all comparable epic poems.

Because of the clear parallel for us at this point, also of interest is the Legend of the Holy Grail, which developed around the same time and in the same geographical regions as the Gothic cathedrals, and which illustrates the same principles with similar symbols, only in another form. The Grail is some kind of vessel which has to be found and which, in its symbolic appearance, is described at one time as a large gem, or at another time as a vessel fashioned from pure gold, studded with gems, filled with supernatural bright light. The actual Grail here again lies hidden in the individual, the searcher. Parsifal—"he who strides through the valley"—finds, after a long search in the outside, the solution in the inside, in himself.

The Legend of the Holy Grail as well as the construction of the cathedral go back possibly to the Knights Templar; it is certain that both have a common source in the inner self of all human beings. The similarity in the symbolism is unmistakable. The roses as well as the Grail develop their strength in connection with light that radiates from them; both initiate the search from the outside and conclude it in the inside, the center. The twelve or twenty-four knights of King Arthur are seated at a round table, in the center of which the rose is depicted (at least on the one at Winchester, which you will find illustrated on the next page), and the seeker will first be sent to search in the outside, although the solution lies in their midst, surrounded by knights.

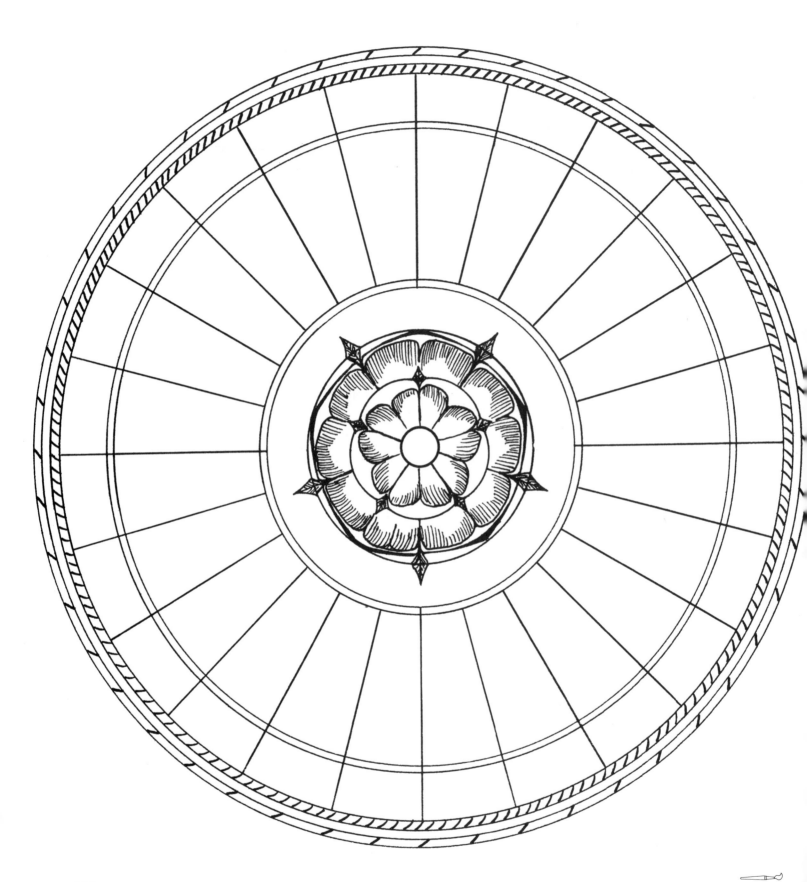

Finally, after a long wandering through a labyrinth of difficulties, one of the knights, precisely that Parsifal who took the path into the depths, asks the right question about the shadow: "What do you lack, uncle?" At the end of the search for the Grail, he receives the familiar answer, "The king and the country are one," that leads back again to the unity. Outside and inside are one, king and country are one, but that can only be realized from the center—inwardly. It is the same in the rose windows: in the outer space (the periphery) the light is colorful, because it is still missing parts of the unity; only toward the center does it then become "more whole."

In the old wheel-windows that was even more evident. In the center is the pure, white, and thus complete light; in the periphery light and stone-structures mix. That might be nice to look at, but in that there is no solution. The periphery, the world of the appearances, only gets its meaning out of the one center.

Also evident is the similarity of the symbols table and rose window as images of the universe, whether around the one center are arranged in groups the twelve knights of the Round Table, the twelve signs of the zodiac, the twelve Apostles, the four elements or four Evangelists, the four rivers of Paradise or the eight winds, the seven liberal arts, or the vices and virtues. The emphasis is always on the dance around the one center.

So we come once again to the labyrinth, because it not only inspired the Bishop of Chartres to dance, but from all parts of the world we have heard legends and stories about dances through the labyrinths, dances sacred and profane. After all, most dances imitate this circular or spiral form, as we have already observed in the waltz.

In this form there is a strange fascination. Most people enjoy it (we think again of Ferris wheels and merry-go-rounds), and it, as we see in the ritual Dhikr of the dervishes and similarly in serpentine dances of so-called primitives, can lead even further into religious ecstasy and to the final detachment from this world.

But this happens in the center. That secret, which is concealed in the circular movement, we still today find in widely divergent connections. Very rarely is it experienced consciously, but it always has its effect, and there is something thrillingly inspiring and ritualistic about it—starting with the pirouette of the ice skaters, up to the dance that weaves around the maypole and in old times around the tree of life, from the small pocket-toy labyrinth, into the center of which children try to place a ball, to the Corrida,

where the toreador stirs the bull into a spiral movement which becomes tighter and tighter, in the center of which the bull becomes completely calm, and then (in the ideal case) the one thrust into the center succeeds.

Behind each of these dances around the center there is the same pattern. Károly Kerényi states that in the labyrinths it must have had a powerful effect, for they were ordered destroyed in many cathedrals, because it was no longer possible to ward off the playing and dancing children. The labyrinth as original-image of life is effective simply through its existence.

We can view life as a Mandala, analogous to the rose window or the labyrinth, because it corresponds in its course with the original vibration of every creation, with the initial expansion and the subsequent contraction, with the way there and back and its turning point in between—all expressed perfectly in each breathing cycle.

We find the same thing, psychologically much more demanding, in the great medieval poem of the Holy Grail by Wolfram von Eschenbach. In this epic Parsifal, after his first disastrous visit to the Castle of the Grail, reaches that turning point, and from then on he has to experience his life once again in retrospect—this time, more consciously. In the rose windows we find a clear parallel to the journey told in the fable of the Grail. In each rose the actual, the essential, comes to life in another dimension, namely in the original point, which cannot be perceived with the conventional senses. Out of this everything emerges, including the creation of the rose, which becomes more and more substantial until it finally solidifies in the darkness of the stone wall—where the vision turns around and is again being pulled back to the center.

Parsifal's life can be understood only symbolically, as an impetuous departure and finally purified homecoming. At the first climax of the Legend of the Holy Grail, he arrives at his crossroad, the turning point of his life, where he has to go within himself; he has to experience his life consciously backwards in order to "become again as a little child."

Only late in his journey can he finally recognize the secret of the Grail, which alone can heal the wounded king Amfortas and his sad and depressed empire (the Creation): "The king and his country are one." In other words, the empire (the Creation) is mirror of the One King and corresponds with him in everything. Microcosm is macrocosm, goes our seemingly so simple parable.

It is clearly stressed that Parsifal begins his path as a child. His mother, Herzeloide, tried to keep him in the empire of the children (in the unity), in order to spare herself and him from further "suffering of the heart," which the death of Parsifal's father (the knight Gachmuret) and his brothers, also knights, had caused outside in the world (Creation). But for Parsifal it is important to go out and to "pass through the center." He has to grow up, but only to reach the turning point of greatest darkness (after he had been expelled from the Castle of the Grail), and from here on to retrace his steps, in order to recognize the course of the whole and finally to rediscover the unity.

So that path out of the center point of the rose leads into the darkness. The light gets lost more and more on this path, the colors become darker, the path takes one into the lead of the frames and finally the stone structures, which become more and more massive. The path ends in the lightless wall. Each path out of the unity leads into this lightless situation and thus to a possible turning point, the "catastrophe" the purpose of which is only to make possible the way back into the light, into the unity.

In our time, when we have lost the understanding of the symbol and to a great extent the ability to draw parallels from our own experiences, it may seem more difficult to recognize the symbols that could point our way. On the conscious, physical level, these original images of life are being less portrayed in art. But still, when we take a closer look, it is apparent that the symbols unconsciously slip in again, as if we could not manage without them.

Thus we still find in the course of individual life cycles exactly the same symbolism that the Legend of the Holy Grail conveys to us—only today we call it (for example) midlife crisis, and we face it with astonishing helplessness. This so-called midlife crisis is nothing else but this same turning point—the same time of introspection that Parsifal experiences when he wakes up in the morning in the deserted Castle of the Holy Grail—the situation when we, coming out of the bright light of the origin, reach the lightless stone wall that surrounds the rose.

Let's have a closer look at this sociological phenomenon of the midlife crisis. It appears less related to the comparative (outer) abundance in the middle of our lifespan and more to our essential (inner) advancement: often when we have achieved the power we sought, and have satisfied our material ambitions—yes, then, when one actually could be the happiest person, instead one becomes sad, depressed, down.

What is it that depresses one, if not the feeling that now all goals have been reached yet the emptiness remains? But through his dilemma one arrives at a very decisive point. Into our time of depression and darkness, the light of realization can be born, so that there is an opportunity for a turnaround, for self-analysis.

As a parallel, the redeeming light of this world, Christ, is being born each year at the time of the greatest darkness, in the night of commemoration of the winter solstice. This night is the distinguished, the consecrated, and thus the most important night of the year, although the light is at its weakest and seems to be lost. And it is in the "night of mankind"—man's darkest hours—that Jesus Christ is expected to return.

Thus the crisis in midlife, whenever that might occur in each individual's time, is the most important one, because it offers the chance to realize that it is time for introspection. "Truly I tell you, if you do not become like a little child, you will never enter the kingdom of heaven. . . ." We hear this message but do not absorb it; we still try to take the easiest way and, as usual, to deal only with externals. Or we misunderstand the message and suddenly become childish again, turn into colorful late-hippies, try to make ourselves young again in our external appearance through clothes, fashion, and cosmetics, or to prove our youth to ourselves by looking for a new, young partner.

Just like all purely external attempts to work things out, these, luckily, are somewhat pathetic and end in disappointments. "Luckily," because in these pathetic attempts lies the chance of discovering that transformation just does not work like this.

Once again it is the disappointment that ends an attempt at self-deception. However, let's not underestimate disappointments—they are an integral part of the same pattern: they are the end of a path which led into deception, and they lead us out of it. We could just as well celebrate the end of the deception. We live, according to the Eastern and esoteric conception, in a world of the deceptions of the *Maya*, and each disappointment thus lifts the veil of the *Maya* a bit more.

On the opposite page you find the labyrinth of Amiens. Try, through painting or reflection, or however you like, to find in it your personal meaning. Meditate about it, create your own life on the basis of this meditation.

147

✦ THE WAY HOME—TURNING BACK ✦

The idea of the turning back and, even more specifically, of the way home, has its roots in Christian doctrine, and thus a misunderstanding might be responsible for the banishment of labyrinths from the churches. For example, in the square labyrinth of Orléanville, we find in the center, and thus in the goal, the words *sancta ecclesia*. According to Jean Hani[1] the labyrinths portray images of the world, in the center of which the Holy City, the New Jerusalem, is situated. This is interesting because also the Gothic cathedrals want to be images of the New Jerusalem, and their roses thus become windows of the Holy City through which we can enter.

It is exactly this entering (introspection) and homecoming into one's own center that the labyrinth wants to bring closer to us. It is the same motif which we find in the parable of the lost son; and also in that Kabbalistic idea about the fallen angel, Lucifer, in the New Testament according to John the Baptist, who preaches repentance and starting anew; and in the story of the transformation of Saul to Paul.

In each pilgrimage this is the theme. One starts a journey in the outside world with the wish to experience something internal. At the goal, which practically always is an external representation of something important that is internal (for the most part, a place to remind us of a former mystery of faith that took place here), one turns around and goes back home. Classical roads of pilgrimage, like the one to Santiago de Compostela, lead straight westward, thus following the sun on its way home. The journey back home consequently then leads eastward, facing the new light. And typically these roads are much older than Christianity: human beings have followed these (external and internal) paths forever.

Parsifal has to repent on his way back; he has to make good on all mistakes that through lack of awareness he made on the outward journey. On his return travels he must recognize his Karma, which he brought on himself on his way there, and he has to redeem it. He has to consciously neutralize the detachment from the unity (symbolized by his mother, Herzeloide).

In our symbols it is important and clearly recognizable that the detachment was not wrong, it was a vital requirement for the way home. It is fitting that Parsifal rebels and goes away—the father (God) loves the lost then returned son more than the good, obedient son who stayed home. And Christ does not say: "If you do not *remain* like a little child," but precisely: "If you do not *become* like a little child. . . ." Considering this, it may astonish less that the Kabbalists call the fallen angel Lucifer God's favorite angel.

Thus the labyrinth and the Legend of the Holy Grail show us almost more distinctly than the rose windows that the Creation does not need our improvements. Whatever we meet in the form of detours or obstacles has its meaning, after all, even if we cannot at first perceive this easily in the labyrinth of life.

---

1. Jean Hani. *O Simbolismo do Templo Cristão*. Lisbon: Colecção Esfinge, 1981.

◆ TURNING BACK TIME ◆

Now we want to do an exercise so that you can practice this turning back in time and extend it at pleasure, when you play with the different time-rhythms.

We begin with a day. In the evening, after you have lived through the light part of the day and lie in bed, go back in time, in order to more consciously experience the shady side of the day, the night, as time for introspection. Therefore you go backwards through time. Starting out in the here and now (in bed), you experience the day once again in reverse this time with more detachment and conscious purpose. When you have arrived at the morning, you once again experience the mood in which you began this day. In the course of time you will realize that, from the beginning, course and end are determined.

Then you go one more step back, to where you were still asleep; and you go on dreaming where you stopped last night. Whether or not you presently find this a likely possibility is less important than the open-mindedness to give it a try. If, though, you completely preclude it, it is truly out of the question for you.

If in the course of time you will practice this technique, you can also examine longer intervals retrospectively: a week—a month—a year—ten years—a lifetime, etc.[2]

---

2. It is not wise according to our experiences to go back further than to the time of birth without help.

◆ ILLUSIONS ◆

Almost all our deceptions begin with the external eyes, and only the inner vision sets us free again. Like no other sense-organ the eye can help us to unveil the illusions in the inside, with which it misleads us in the outside.

One hundred million visual cells see innumerable different impressions, and each of these visual points transmits its information via the optic nerve into the brain, and there, from these one hundred million individual pieces of information, an image is created. This image, which we now see, is not on the outside, but clearly on the inside; not even on the retina, but only in the brain. Thus we do not actually look out into the world, but the world looks inside us. The images are always inside. But whether what we see there relates to what there "really" is seems rather unlikely—it is more likely that each donkey sees its own world and each ant sees its own world.

But even if we, for once, accept the outside world as real, it can still reveal its character of illusion to us.

Let's look at a Mandala, a wheel, that turns. From a certain speed on, in our perception, it suddenly starts to move in the opposite direction (as can be seen in carriage wheels in old movies). And then suddenly it is standing completely still, although in reality it is spinning very fast. Each film is based on this illusion—but the figures which move in the film "in reality" are standing absolutely still in their individual frames. And don't we each night view the most varied films in our dreams, which suddenly in the morning do not exist anymore? Are you sure that what begins with the awakening in the morning is not another film as well? Because what is it that we see, after all? It is all things that do not really exist, as physics proves to us. Everything that we regard as a solid object is instead vibrating energy—only it vibrates so fast that we simply cannot see that.

Of all individual sciences, physics has advanced furthest, to the limits of our universe, and it is about to make statements which could just as well stem from any timeless holy book: for example, the statement that everything is connected with everything else, or that everything is vibration and, therefore, energy.

If everything, including each atom, is energy, so also, according to physics, the human being is just an energy phenomenon—a vibrating Mandala. This knowledge exists throughout the world in every language. The Indians have perhaps most clearly expressed it in their Chakra system. Alongside the spinal column, in an energy channel, the Sushumna, seven energy centers or Chakras, are located. Chakra means "wheel" or "circle," and Chakras are mostly portrayed in forms of flowers (as the lotus)—Mandalas of energy. All together they envelop the human being in a globe-shaped field of vibration. However, in this image the center-point is developed into an axle, the spine, which in the big Mandala of the macrocosm would correspond to the axis of the earth.

In other cultures there are other names and slight deviations, but in the end they all deal with the same energy phenomenon contemplated through different cultural eye-glasses. Thus to the Chinese the circuit lines which connect energy centers are known as Meridians, while the Indians call them Nadis. Instead of seven Chakras, the Tibetans have only five, because they have combined two pairs; and the Hopi Indians count only the topmost five Chakras of the Hindu system. The Tibetans, for example, visualize the energy as entering at the top Chakra and then descending, while the Indians let it rise up from the Muldhara, the lowest Chakra. Here the same universal process is being contemplated from different points of view. In each Mandala the process is visible: The law of the living center, from which everything is born and into which everything goes back again . . . from the center to the center or, as the Indians say: from here to here.

Now provide the human-being-Mandala on page 29 with the seven energy centers in Mandala form.

Combine the seven centers to a single energy-image, to the aura-image of the human being.

Then paint the Chakra drawing of the third eye on page 151 as symbol of the deeper introspection and perspective.

Colors of the original:

The outer two lotus leaves: brilliant light-blue

The circle: white

The Lingam in the middle: light-blue

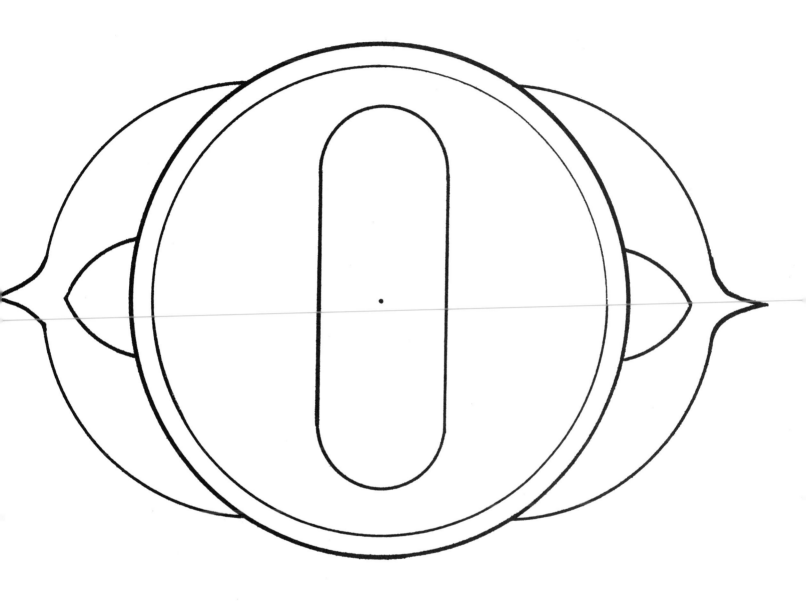

The depiction of the fourth, or heart, Chakra brings us elements that we already know from the Christian art of the Middle Ages, like the hexagram and the symbolism of the twelve. The two interpenetrating triangles here stand for the balance between the polar forces of the universe. The upper one represents Shiva and thus the male principle, the lower one the Goddess Shakti, the female. This Chakra (through its position in the human body between the three upper and the three lower Chakras) also represents the balance of the energy forces in the center, the heart area.

The energy which is flowing in the Sushumna is what the Indians call Kundalini, snake-force. According to their belief, the Kundalini-snake lies rolled up in three and a half spirals in the lower Chakra (Muldhara), where it is waiting for its resuscitation. The expression *Kundalini* developed from the Sanskrit word *Kundal,* which means "spiral." Thus also this circle closes again. So, according to Eastern belief, not only does the external energy of the macrocosm/ universe move in spirals, but, by analogy, so flows the inner energy of the microcosm/human being.

Color instructions for the fourth Chakra according to Eastern tradition: grey-green hexagram in the white circle surrounded by twelve vermilion lotus petals.

Only now and then in our culture do we encounter the knowledge about the spiral-shaped flow of energy. In ancient times, however, it seems to have been alive in the West, if, for example we think of the staff of Aesculapius, the symbol of the Greek doctors. Here a single snake (energy) winds itself around a rod (spine) in *three and a half turns* upwards. At that time the snake was considered to be holy, and in the temples of Aesculapius snakes were kept and worshipped as gods.

Below you see the staff of Hermes, which, with its two snakes, the black and the white, additionally symbolizes the polarity, which in the center, where the two snakes meet, becomes a point, the Divine Center. The staff of Hermes still today is a sign for us Western doctors. However, the knowledge about energy-flow was lost, and we are just discovering it anew.

Use this page to let your own energy-Mandala come into existence. In your personal perception, which form matches the flow of the energy? And which color does it require?

MANDALAS OF NATURE

The Mandala represents the middle. It belongs neither to the East nor to the West. In the end we can find it only in our own center. The path there begins in the periphery (the outside), and while we follow it, we will locate Mandalas in a wide variety of cultures, discovering that their differences will be merely external: i.e., in the periphery. In the center of the Mandala all differences neutralize each other and they unite as one.

All cultures and human beings are part of nature. We also remain, despite technical advancement and all of our progress, embedded in nature and dependent on it. Nature, though, is full of Mandalas, and thus it cannot be overlooked that in the truest sense of the word they are universal—the **one** in all the different expressions.

In the center of each natural rose grow its seeds, known to us from Christian symbolism. Looking at seeds of different plants, we again find Mandalas—most distinctly in the fruits, the globular shape of almost all of them surrounding the one core, the one center. The first secures the plant's existence through endless cycles of development. But even the sectional view of each individual blade, each stalk, each branch, and each stem shows a Mandala. Here you see the annual rings of a tree—a Mandala that, similar to a horoscope, combines time and space in a picture.

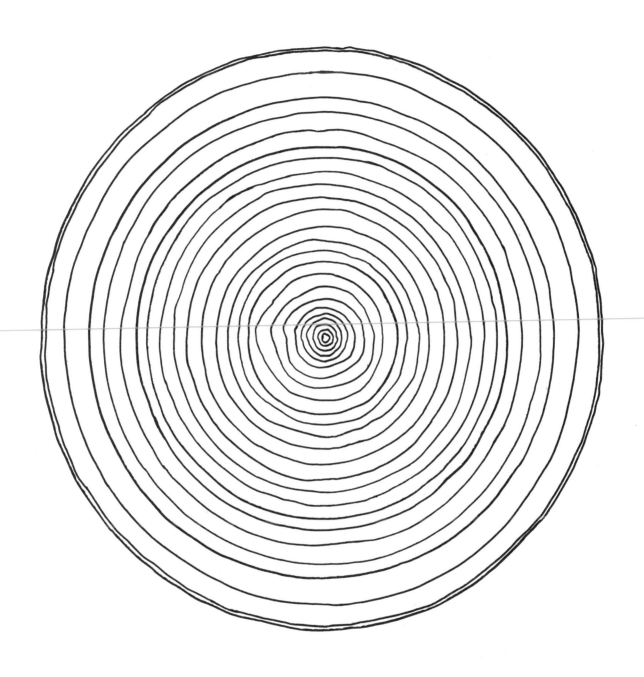

The rose windows are created according to the shape of a flower, and the window-roses are based partially on the same principle that determines the arrangement of the petals and the young shoots of the plants. It is only surprising that science took so many centuries to discover this principle. Maybe here we should—as in many other cases—talk a little about "rediscovery."

Now we want to rediscover the flowers—and in each flower the Mandala.

The row of Mandalas is infinite—without end. The more we learn to see, the more we will find. An obvious association is also the spider's web with its Mandala structure.

You can now transform it into your personal colorful spider's web.

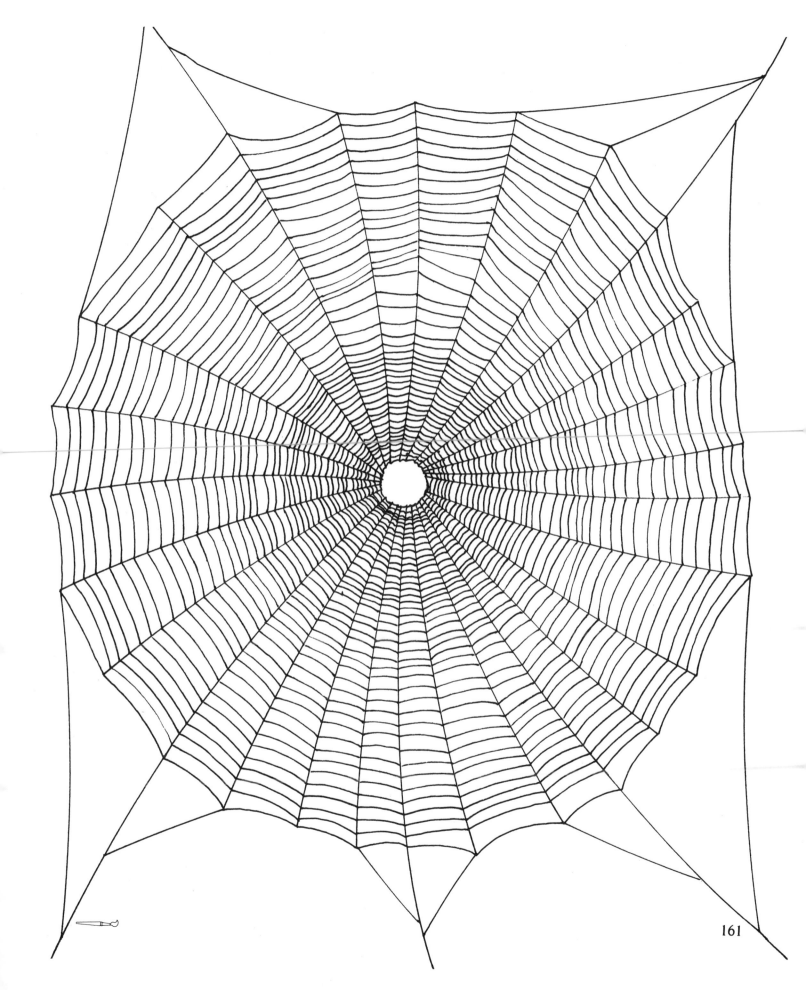

• THE SPIDER IN US •

Although it is a perfect Mandala, the spider's web at first engenders unpleasant feelings. After all, it shows the nature of the spider (and its web) so clearly that we unconsciously see more in it than we wish to. Each person lives in a similar web, which ties one with innumerable threads to his/her world! This web has first to be recognized, then accepted, and finally consciously experienced, in order to redeem it. Probably the spider is such a nauseating symbol because it reminds us of our being wrapped up in the world, our being attached and tied up in many ways. Probably also, because it reveals to us our perfidiously lurking way of catching other creatures in this web and letting them struggle also. While watching them, we forget how we ourselves are hanging on struggling.

The symbolism continues. The spider, too, takes advantage of the illusion that its web does not exist at all. It has to be so thin that it becomes invisible, and only at the moment of dying does the web become reality to the captive. Thus we, too, repress this web until, facing death, we cannot deny it any longer. The Mandala of the spider's web is like any other Mandala image of this creation, and we are like the insects that have been caught somewhere in the periphery, i.e., in the creation that materialized. The more and more unconsciously we romp around in this world, the more we get entangled in this net.

Now paint the Mandala of the spider—since it is a Mandala—and do it nicely, maybe occupying yourself a little bit at the same time with your own spider-nature—possibly even learning to love it. And then also meditate about the web, which you should create beforehand, and feel from that how you carry the nature of the web in yourself.

Of course at first you cannot find the web in yourself, and others are not allowed to discover it at all—assuming, so subtle is the web, that nobody sees it. Now take the courage to look at it nevertheless, because the less you like spiders and spiders' webs the more certain the web is to be there.

The outer shells of many mussels, the shape of the sea urchins and of the anemones, of the corals—all are Mandalas, including the shells of the snails, which remind us of the original nebular whirl, as well as of the labyrinths.

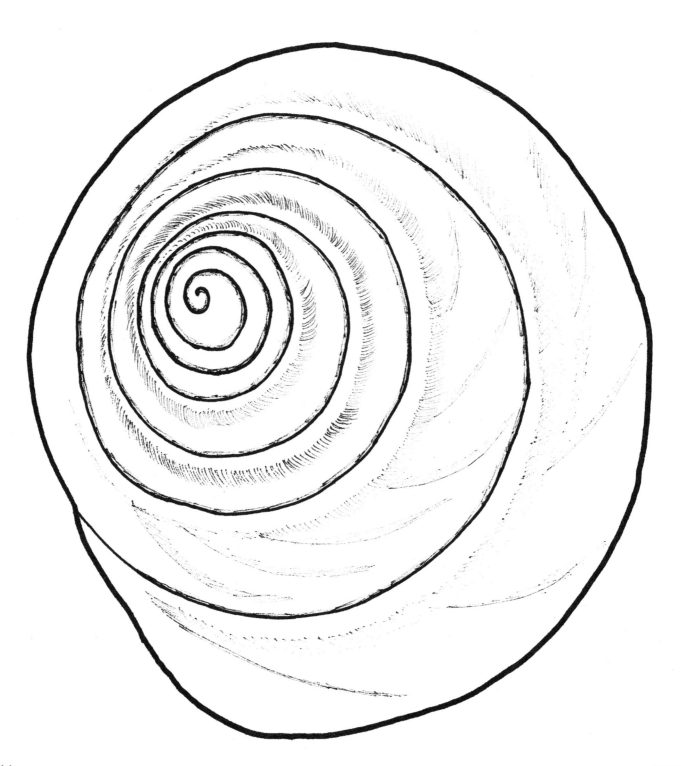

Out of one of these Mandalas, namely a mussel, according to the legend, Venus, the Goddess of Love, was born.

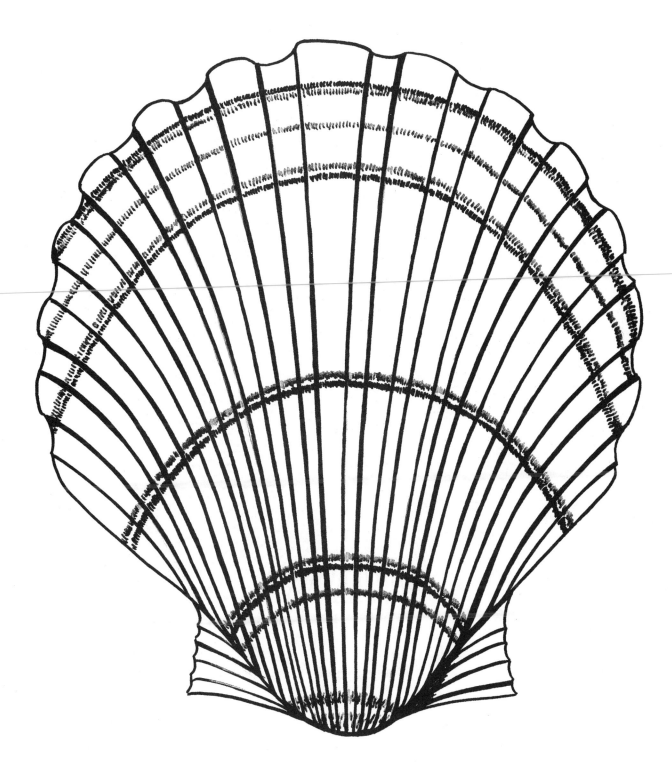

The mussel-Mandala is not only the birthplace of love, but also of pearls, glimmering in the spectrum hues of mother of pearl. Those symbols of tears and of the Resurrection—they are Mandalas as well. Already in their three-dimensional global shape we recognize the glimmering Mandala. This impression becomes even clearer when we cut through the middle of a pearl.

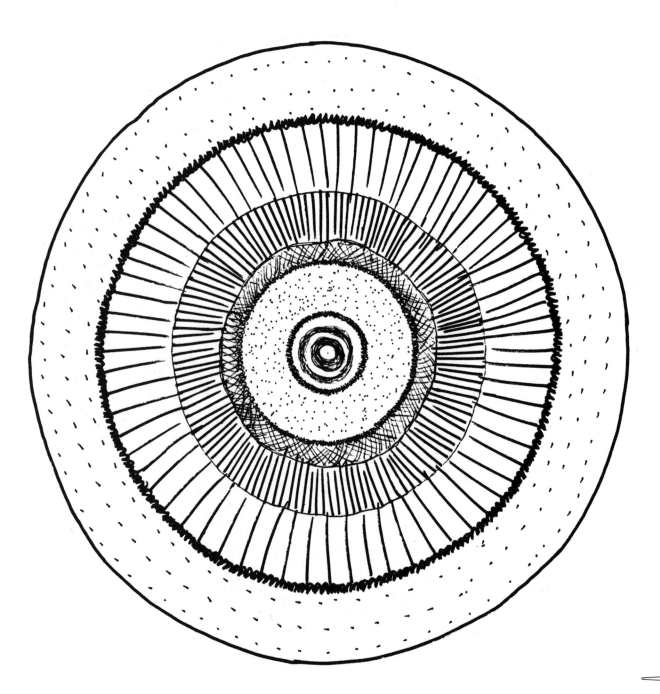

The early dwellings of human beings often had Mandala shapes. Today we still see it in the African kraal or the tepees of the American Indians. We, on the other hand, moved into rectangular houses, which also externally reveal our materially oriented center of gravity. The religious sites and the houses of God throughout all times, until today, have usually been arranged in Mandala shapes. From above, all churches in the rectangular style of a basilica (and likewise the Greek Orthodox temples) form exactly the basic shape of the Tibetan Yantra: the combination of block (square for the worldly) and globe in the dome above (globe and circle represent the divine).

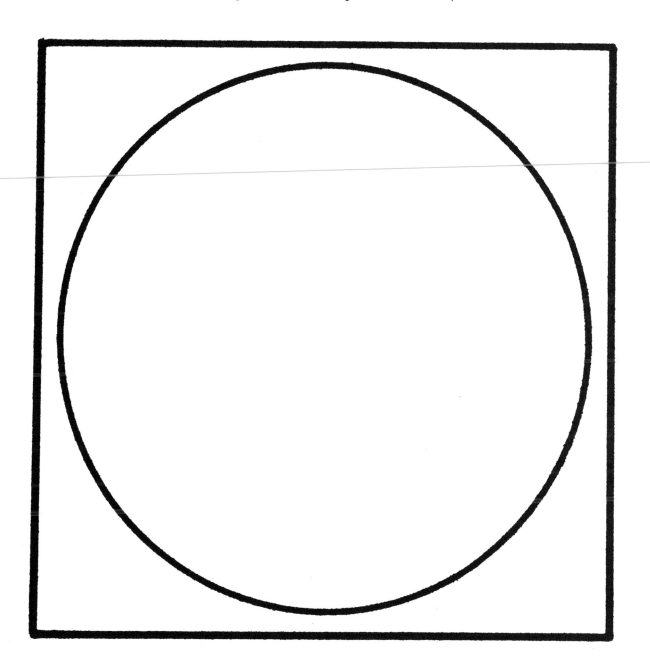

While today we have long forgotten the connection to the Mandala, it continues to exist in form. Our modern theaters and circus arenas are round because, as we can still see from the word "theater," they were originally sacral places. The word "theater" contains the two Greek words Theos = God and Jatros = doctor; it originally meant something like "a place where one is being healed through the meeting with the divine." Our heathenish ancestors used the Mandala principle for their holy places, as we can still see impressively at Stonehenge, that gigantic calendar-observatory of the Druids and their ancestors. Religious buildings of the East, like the pagodas and the stupas, are still today being very consciously built and used according to this pattern. The pyramids of Egypt and of the Mayans show the same principle.

The architect Le Corbusier built a small step-pyramid beside "his" church, Notre Dame du Haut, near Ronchamps.

Human beings have always had the feeling of being closer to the gods on the peak of high mountains. And in India one may go, in fact, to the peak of a mountain to the center of a Mandala. The cross on top of the peak makes us more than ever aware of this. From the perspective of the gods, Meru, the Holy Mountain of the Indians, with its symmetrical form, has the following shape.

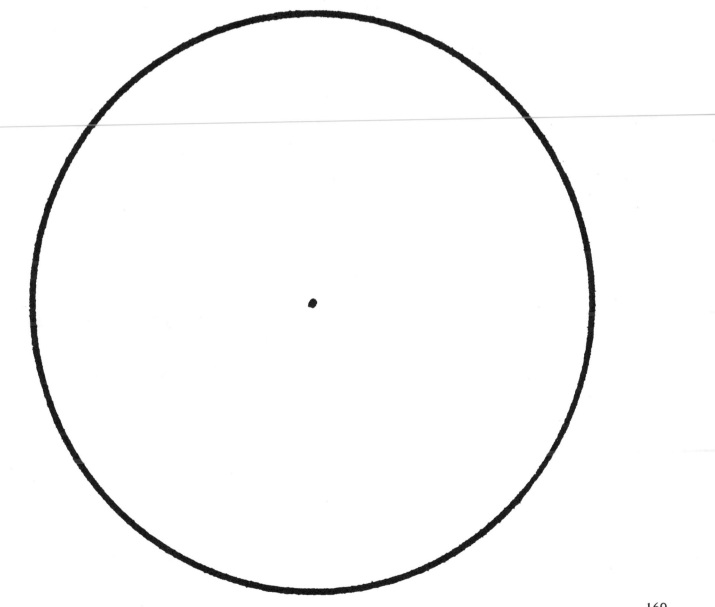

"What the body is for the soul and the oil for the lamp, that is a Yantra for the divinity." In the East one deals with Yantras accordingly carefully, just as with a dwelling of God. This idea might seem naive at first sight—but only at first sight—because in the East it is still believed that each Yantra, because it is God's dwelling, represents an energy field. On the basis of this concept of meditating on energy, the Yantra turns into a complex, total ritual of worship of one's God. And this ritual advances the spiritual development of the worshipper.

In the linkage of object and subject lies a fascinating secret, which the East can give us as a present. Because of this indissoluble connection, the religion there is less likely to decay into an external process that does not involve the true believer anymore. Eastern religion always begins with the seeking person, and is therefore inseparably connected with exercises and techniques that further his development, so that he recognizes God in himself.

In Christianity we still have the same theory, for example, in that sentence of Christ's: "Because truly, I tell you, God's kingdom of heaven lies in you." But the succors to experience this sentence got lost, and so this goal gradually disappeared. Yes, for some Christians these words of Christ contain a revelation.

The East, on the other hand, has always preserved its own tools to achieve the experience of God, and to these tools, besides many others, belongs the Yantra. Each Yantra creates solely through its form, which is placed into the empty space (that energy field or field of force) that automatically contains the diversity as well. The Egyptian pyramids and the cathedrals and especially their rose windows represent a similar phenomenon. Based on this conception of the quality of a place or space, the temples of the East are built in Mandala shape, because they are sacred regions which separate the divine from the profane world through their outside boundaries.

On the opposite page you see the ground plan of a pagoda.

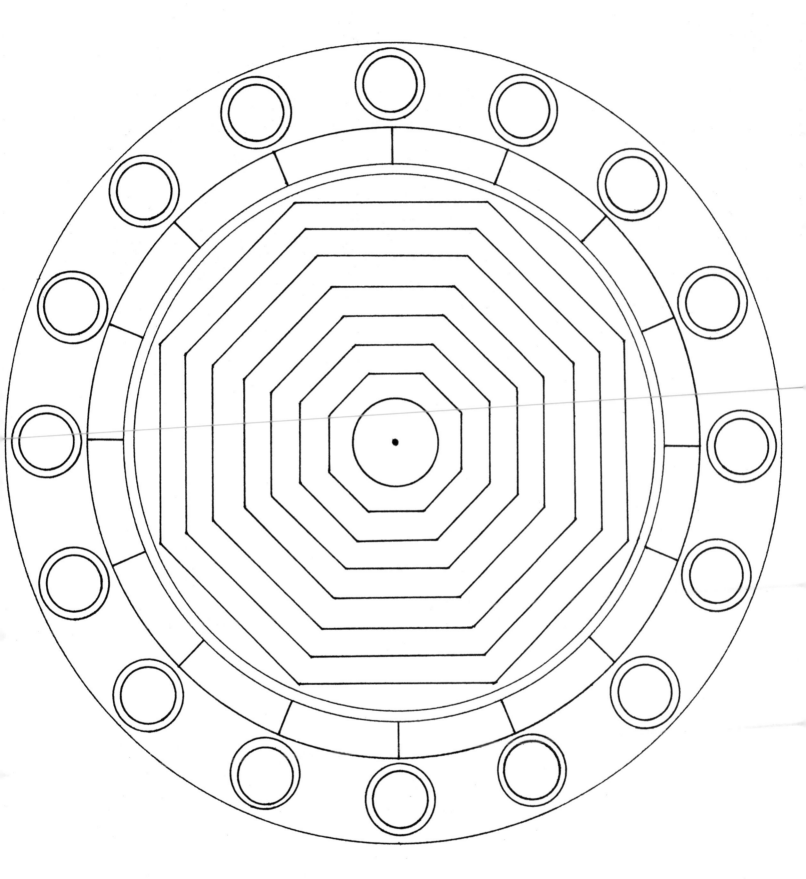

Eastern ideas about the formation and structure of a Holy Space are largely congruent with our experiences with the rose windows. The East calls the center, the spaceless point, "bindu." The bindu is the original point of every creation, the point that contains the One and the totality on a transcendental level and becomes the germinating point of the material creation.

In the human being the bindu center-point is in the sixth Chakra, which lies between and just above the eyebrows, at the spot of the so-called "third eye." During the Yantra-meditation, this center in the meditating person and the center of the Yantra are being joined through concentration.

As we will see later, the Gypsies know a very simple meditation that leads the consciousness, as if on its own, onto this spot.

To the Yantra-meditation also belongs a so-called "Mantram," a spiritually oriented syllable or sound, which also contributes to center the consciousness. The usage of sounds is not astonishing in any way, since the Yantra has a certain form, certain colors, and a certain sound as its energy-pattern. We sometimes use this combination of words: color-tone, sound-color (timbre). One of the most important Mantrams, which corresponds with the original vibration, is "Om." In the East one deals very carefully with the Mantram. It is never mentioned loudly or in a profane connection, since it would affect the human being on the most refined levels and would be damaged by coarseness.

Also you shall deal sensitively with the Yantra. The painting all by itself will open you entirely to its vibration.

173

◆ MEDITATION ◆

Each meditation technique aims at the same thing, at the same center, and still there are many different ways to proceed, just as there are innumerable Mandalas but only one center. There are no right or wrong Mandalas; there are no right or wrong meditation techniques. An argument about it simply misses the point. An argument is entertainment for the intellect. Everybody should, if he/she wants to, look for the technique which suits him/her at the moment—you already have to know some possibilities. In my experience the *kind* of technique is less important than its regularity, because only regular practice leads us to the first decision: intellect or inner self.

Via the clarification of the terms "concentration" and "Mantram," we now want to feel our way to a technique that, in my belief, is well suited for the experience of Mandalas—for Mandala-meditation. If you have developed another taste or still are developing one, follow your own. To repeat what we have said: Do not let yourself be *restricted* by suggestions, but *stimulated*. In the word "concentration" are two keys that clarify to us what this is about: "centration" (a process that focuses one on the task) and "concentric" (having a common center). For example, water into which a stone has fallen forms concentric circles. Thus concentration is doubly connected with the Mandala. We need only to open up to the Mandala, to contemplate it, then by itself the process of the concentration begins.

Now there are different Mandalas and thus multiple paths to the center, all of them united by the principle of the center. Let's think again of the labyrinth. Here in the truest sense of the word one has to search with the senses for the path into the center. On the other hand, most of the Mandalas, especially the Tantric Yantras, move one unconsciously toward the center. While, for example, the Western roses even want to encourage this unconscious urge (brought out by the structure, through processes of the intellect in their metaphors that tell the stories), the East in general relies above all on the strength that rests in the pattern.

In this sense each Mantram is, of course, a Mandala, because it falls into the consciousness and there—comparable to the image of the stone falling into the water and its concentric waves—it gradually stops its motion and it becomes less and less perceptible and thus finer. The sole purpose of the Mantram is to orient one toward the center. And with that we come to the next step: the technique of the Mantram-meditation, which shall serve as example of our Mandala-meditation.

One absorbs a Mantram in thought (i.e., one thinks it, hears it, sees it, feels it, whichever or all together) and observes it without strain—one lets it really swing until it comes to a halt, follows it through the different levels of consciousness. If one loses it, or becomes absorbed with other thoughts, then this is all right. One returns effortlessly, almost unintentionally, back to the Mantram and observes it anew: how it gradually sinks into the consciousness and so on, again and again the same cycle between coming and going. The Mantram essentially is a sound—like "Om." You concentrate on a Mantram in the same way that you concentrate on the sound of a gong or of a sound-bowl or a bell (all three Mandalas in their shapes; a Yantra is a visual image, a pattern, of a sound).

In the Mandala-meditation we simply follow the impression that the shape of the Mandala leaves in our inner self, until we lose this impression (perhaps because of distracting thoughts), and then we begin anew again, look at our Mandala, until we again lose ourselves in our thoughts and come back again, etc. . . . in the hope that we, for once, fall through into the center-point. It is this hope that, surprisingly, holds us tight and hinders us. As necessary as hope is at the beginning, we nevertheless will have to overcome it at one point. Only if meditation takes place without any intentions, demands, expectations, or hopes—really without purpose—can "it" happen, and we reach the center that we long for.

175

The greatest part of our life is controlled by the desire to understand what is happening. We want to act reasonably and want to be insightful. But only in the center of the Mandala does insight really become possible: insight into the wheel of life, into worldly logic, into the Creation.

As far as there can be a goal of the Yantra-meditation at all, it is the following: that Yantra and observer become **one** in the bindu, the point of origin (the third eye).

The geometric structures on which the Yantras are based correspond (as already the identical vision of the center leads us to assume) with the structures which are already well known to us in the roses. The East, in addition, has preserved theory and system in the making of its Mandalas.

The center is created by the bindu, which corresponds with the element Akasha, i.e., spirit. Subsequent material levels are created by four other elements, or "Tattwas." To each Tattwa corresponds a form-symbol. The five basic forms are: the point for the Akasha principle, the circle for the air-Tattwa, the triangle for fire, the increasing half-moon for water, the square for earth. Out of these five basic oscillations was made the entire Creation, and thus also all Yantras.

On the opposite empty page from these basic forms create a Mandala, and experience through it the quality of the individual symbols.

For the people of the East, the making of a Yantra is a ritual. The building of temples becomes divine service. Temples always correspond to a Yantra-form, mostly the Vastu-Purusha Yantra, which portrays the actual nature of the human being, i.e., the divine Self. Thus the art of the East keeps its religious purpose and consequently promotes the weakening of the Ego in favor of the Self, while in our culture the individuality (and thus in the end the Ego) became motive and the center-point of art. This conflicting understanding of art can also make clear to us some things for our meditation. According to the Eastern understanding, meditation can only "take place." A Western understanding (which emphasizes the Ego, and *places* the artist or the meditating person into the center-point) can never find the center, since it never belongs to the Ego of the individual person, but solely to the impersonal absolute Being—God.

181

The symbolism of numerology is analogously valid for the Yantras, the basic pattern of which is the circle in the square, i.e., the divine, the infinite, in the midst of the finite, the material. Special features of Yantras are the frequently appearing four portals, which are created by opposite-facing Swastikas, one above the other, that form the basic shape. Behind that the symbolism of polarity is concealed. The left-turning (destructive) and the right-turning (constructive) forces belong together on the level of the material world. Out of their balanced cooperation are created the portals that lead into the inside, into the holy One.

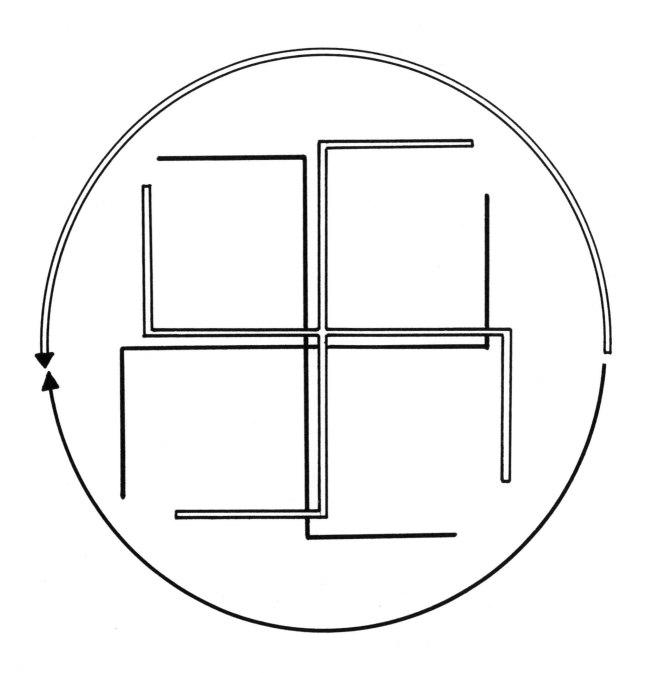

In Yantras we rediscover many things which we already found in the cathedrals: The Indians know the wheel of fortune as well; they too use labyrinths for concentration; and, like the American Indians, they use Mandalas for healing purposes. Another strange parallel is to be found in a temple in honor of the Sun God Surya in Orissa (India). This temple consists of three Yantras of equal area: a circle, a square, and a rectangle. These three geometric forms, also equal in area, play a major role in the layout of the Cathedral of Chartres.[1] The Gypsies use exactly these three forms for their consecration gardens; and in some legends of the Holy Grail it is said that the Grail rested on precisely three such panels.

Even if Eastern and Western temples seem to be completely different externally, the principles lying behind them are nevertheless in accordance—even in the West, where we do not understand them at all. Let us remember that the old churches—whether they had as basic pattern the Greek cross of the Romantic movement or the Latin cross of the Gothic—had the altar always at the crossing point of the two beams, so to speak in the center of meaning of the church. We find the same thing in the Indian culture: the innermost shrine, the Holy of Holies, the dwelling of the most important god, is always in the center of the Yantra. An example here is the layout of the Barabadur Stupa in Indonesia: a perfect Yantra. It includes an entire temple city, which was built in the eighth century on a holy mountain. The faithful went on a symbolic pilgrimage that led them higher and higher and at the same time closer to the center, while they circled around the Holy of Holies (the center-point of the mountain and of the temple) in a spiral (compare the symbolic path through the horoscope on page 93). The higher and the closer they came to the center, the more shapeless became the innumerable Buddha statues that bordered their path, by which should be indicated that at the last, knowledge withdraws from each form.

With a saying of just this Buddha who lived for the doctrine of emptiness, of Nirvana, we want to bring to a temporary end the journey to the East: "If you orientate your heart towards the **one** point, nothing will be impossible for you."

1. Compare L. Charpentier. *The Secret of the Cathedral of Chartres.* Cologne: Gaia, 1972.

When you look very closely, you will find on the next, seemingly empty, page nevertheless everything—namely a bindu. From this you now construct again your "own" Mandala, well knowing that it is, just like yourself, expression of the One, which you have in common with all the forms that appear in this Creation.

While doing so this time, you should trace the birth of the Mandala. Maybe close your eyes at first, staying alert, and let the Mandala grow in front of your inner eye. It originates there in any case, whether or not you experience that consciously. While you are constructing it from that bindu, you can close your external eyes again and again, in order to realize the process more clearly with the internal eye. Which tools you want to use is left to your creativity; the degree of exactness you strive for depends on your devotion to structure and harmony. Create the Mandala out of your own unlimited resources of form- and color-elements. This reservoir is unlimited and if you have the opposite impression, it can be due only to limitations, barriers, and shadows, which you have to eliminate before you become boundless. How about beginning right now to jump across these shadows?

As we have seen, there are doors at all four cardinal (compass) points that lead to the inside. We can also use each of our five senses in order to get inside: the experience of each individual sense influences the others at the same time. When we experience a feeling of love while hearing a piece of music or while looking at something pleasing, always the body will feel warm too, the eyes and the voice become soft and loving.

We have devoted ourselves in this book particularly to the vision and we want to come back to the eyes and the vision again. As we have said frequently, there are many paths to the same center. To me the path with open eyes seems to be more suitable for Western people than the one with closed eyes. To close one's eyes means to turn away from the world of the *Maya*, the deception; it means to lock out one's Ego and to seek for the truth in the inside. This would be, for example, the path of asceticism and mysticism.

The path with open eyes has the same goal—to find the one truth—but it uses the world in its task. The world has to be examined in all aspects again and again, and seen through, until the attachment and clinging forms dissolve. This is essentially the path of magic. *The magician has to com-prehend the world, without being ap-prehended by it* (see Glossary, *Magician*). The difference between the two paths can be easily made clear in the Mandala. While the mystic turns directly toward the center and therefore tries to exclude the periphery of the Mandala, it is taking the path *through* this periphery into the center that becomes the magician's task.

Now it certainly is not right to declare one as the Western and the other as the Eastern path—there are both versions in East and West. I personally, after a time of closing my eyes, feel more comfortable with the path of the open eyes. This book is—even if it shall become completely yours—still under my influence, therefore at some places I expect your question: "And now? What next?" The seemingly simple answer: "Contemplate." Do not do anything, do not do everything; contemplate.

Be receptive, be accepting, be open-minded without clinging to the need for answers and without dissociating oneself from the world. Look at the world and realize that it is in (its present) order because that's what is.

Leave that—leave what is calmly—as it is.

And since almost no one is so composed that he/she could let go of everything, we want to turn to the composure and the composed contemplation.

When you are standing in front of a large Mandala, at best a rose window, you can stare into the center, at the center-point, and be conscious almost exclusively of this. This generally is called concentration. In fact it leads to fatigue and brings you very little closer to the goal, the center.

Instead, try, for a change, to observe the rose window, or a comparable-sized Mandala, as a whole. Start by concentrating on the middle. Very gradually, then, begin to expand your horizon until you are aware of the entire Mandala—now you are experiencing everything equally, although the individual detail is less sharp.

Whoever does not succeed at the first attempt should try the following: Form with both hands a kind of a telescope or blinders and look through the opening. Then slowly open your hands until they gradually frame the entire rose. Look at the rose-Mandala as a whole, without clinging to any detail—thus you automatically get more of an overall impression than a sharp picture. To a degree, as your gaze becomes more relaxed and less fixated, so did your thoughts become more relaxed and less fixed on details. Eyes and thoughts and all other senses devote themselves to the experience of the entirety and disengage themselves from the individual elements.

Try this exercise sometime in a church in front of a rose window. If in addition there should be organ music and the scent of incense, these will facilitate your meditation, because you will be thrust into the middle via other senses. You then live more out of your right brain-half, which, after all, is the half better suited for grasping entireties. In time you will succeed more and more easily in grasping a big horizon with a relaxed **soft** look. In case you cannot or do not want to practice in a church, it is also possible at any other place.

"Everything that you need is always there, exactly where you are."

◆ VISUAL EXERCISES ◆

Stretch both arms forward, the palms together. Now sharply look at your hands, then gradually take them apart more and more and follow both hands *at the same time* with your eyes. Thus your horizon soon becomes larger and larger. You will realize that it even goes beyond half of your periphery—i.e., you also perceive what is happening behind you, without directly looking behind you. You will also realize that objects now and then double; that is, a thing suddenly divides itself and swims apart directly into two whole, new objects. This experience is entirely normal and is simply based on the fact that the eyes are now not focused on one point, but they are so relaxed that you see the objects with each eye separately. You have only to look sharply and the spook has disappeared, and you see anew one thing, where you have just seen two.

You can very easily expand this exercise by simply holding a pencil or something else in front of you and then, not looking at the pencil, but at something that is some distance behind it, you "see" two pencils. Once you can do that, it is only a small step further to make four things out of two.[2]

To do that you simply hold two pencils 30 to 40 centimeters (12 to 16 inches) away in front of your nose and look into the distance, and already you have four. If you play a little bit with the distances or the eyes, you can let the two inner pencils fall together, so that you now see three instead of four.

Now something astonishing is happening. If you look for some time at your three pencils you will realize that the one in the middle can be seen most distinctly and graphically—although it is just this one which "in reality" does not exist at all.

Then again this is really not so astonishing, because you see this middle pencil with both eyes and the two outer ones with only one eye each. The graphic, spatial vision is created precisely by the fact that we look at something with two eyes which are set apart a bit. The one-eyed person sees everything as flat; he lacks the third dimension which brings depth.

---

2. And it is quite possible that that will not happen so fast—some people have always been able to do this, and others first have to get experience.

In order to experience everything in one book, we need even another step. Just as one can double each thing by looking beyond it onto a level behind it, one can do this by looking onto an imagined level in front of it. You can practice this with a Mandala. In between the T'ai Chi Mandala and your eyes hold a pencil and look at it.

You experience then in the background, soft and somewhat blurred, two Mandalas. Out of the two you can make at first four, and then again three, Mandalas.

The visual exercises are the key to the first secret of the consecration-garden of the Gypsies[3]. This garden consists of two squares combined to form a rectangle which is fenced in by a **violet** thread and which is so large that a person can sit in one of the squares. The Gypsies measure the rectangle with their own step-measurement: one step into the width, two into the length. One square (field) is empty. In the other field there are the three panels of the Grail arranged above each other and in two columns. The Gypsies call these columns the "flowers" of their garden. The colors of these geometrical flowers are red and blue and alternate each time, so that always a red one is next to a blue one, and the polar colors are opposite each other. That sounds much more complicated than it looks.

Paint this garden according to the following instructions:
The doubly outlined geometrical figures: red
The ones outlined with one line: blue
The two large squares: light green
The border, the thread around the garden: violet

3. This garden is more explicitly described and explained in Pierre Derlon's book *Die Gärten der Einweihung* (*The Gardens of Consecration*), Basel: Sphinx, 1978. Furthermore, you will find there many of our symbols, this time from the viewpoint of the Gypsies: for example, the three plates of the Grail, the labyrinth of Chartres, and the spiral.

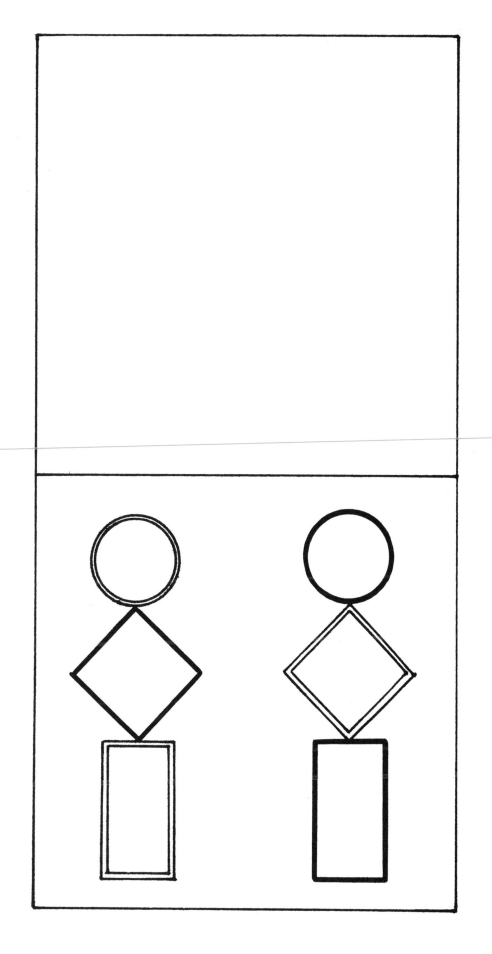

The Gypsy now sits opposite the two flowers (the columns) and composedly looks at them, and they turn into four flowers and then into three, and the flower in the middle is of the one color violet, the color of the harmony of the contrasts of red and blue. It is more graphic and thus livelier than its two polar neighbors. And then these two (the polarity) disappear totally from the Gypsy's vision, which calmly rests on the harmony of the flower in the middle, which exists only in him. His vision is now automatically focused on his third eye, his entire concentration lies in the middle. On the level of the brain he probably is now between two hemispheres.

Now to the second, the actual secret of the garden, which is not dedicated to consecration in vain. So far everything was practice and technique. But if one masters both effortlessly—and that is a prerequisite—one can go on the journey through the flower in the middle and, as the Gypsies do, consecrate oneself into one's own inner world. There is not much to say about this, and what one can say is not the essential. It happens, and if at first nothing is happening, it is good that way too.

The Oriental fairy tales, which tell of flying carpets, teach us that this kind of travelling into the inside can be just as much fun as the journeys into the outside world. If we think about our Gypsy in his garden, we can easily imagine how that Muslim begins to travel and to fly on his prayer carpet, because if we look at the Islamic prayer carpets, we find the same rectangular shape as the consecration-gardens, and the carpets are full of patterns and ornaments, usually in the polar colors of warmth and coldness along with their harmonic cooperation in violet. Practically without exception, these patterns are arranged symmetrically, so that the left and right side have corresponding forms—and soon the journey can begin.

If we look at Oriental prayer carpets even more thoroughly we will realize that frequently a tree of life is woven into the middle (the longitudinal axis), a motif which we know from the Jewish Kabbala and find in many Christian church windows. It is a motif with which Christ is often identified: He said about Himself that He was the vine on which we, the fruit, live. Finally, we find this tree of life at the very beginning, where it grows next to the "tree of the recognition of good and bad" in Paradise. Both trees have their roots in the unity of Paradise.

This way we have come back again to our Western tradition. Possibly also the tree of life formerly served the Kabbalists for similar journeys—its form at least can be sensed. It has a left and a right column (and they are actually called that), which are opposite each other symmetrically and which would, in an exercise similar to those of the Gypsies, create a third, middle column, that would be the one actually alive and essential. Now the tree of life actually has such a middle column, and the spheres in it have, in fact, the function of uniting the two neighboring, outer ones in it and of bringing them into a harmonic balance.

In the drawing on the opposite page we can see that the middle column may be somewhat shifted upwards or downwards—as one wishes—and contains a fourth sphere. Now that does not fit into the described system at all. Maybe it simply means that the uppermost sphere (Kether) is an entirely new level which cannot be "looked into" anymore.

And something else—the name "Kabbala," from which the tree of life stems—indicates that the life-tree served for travelling. Etymologically one still recognizes the relationship to the cavalry, the mounted military troops. We see the similarity in the word "cavalier." Cavalier, in turn, stems from *chevalier,* the horseman-knight. Thus the Kabbalist may have been originally, above all, an inner "active knight."

We had already come across the connection of the ideals of the outer and inner knighthood when we talked about the Knights Templar, whose rules of the order were formulated by its spiritual father, Bernard of Clairvaux, very consciously according to these two ideals; also the Knights of the Grail unite both principles in themselves.

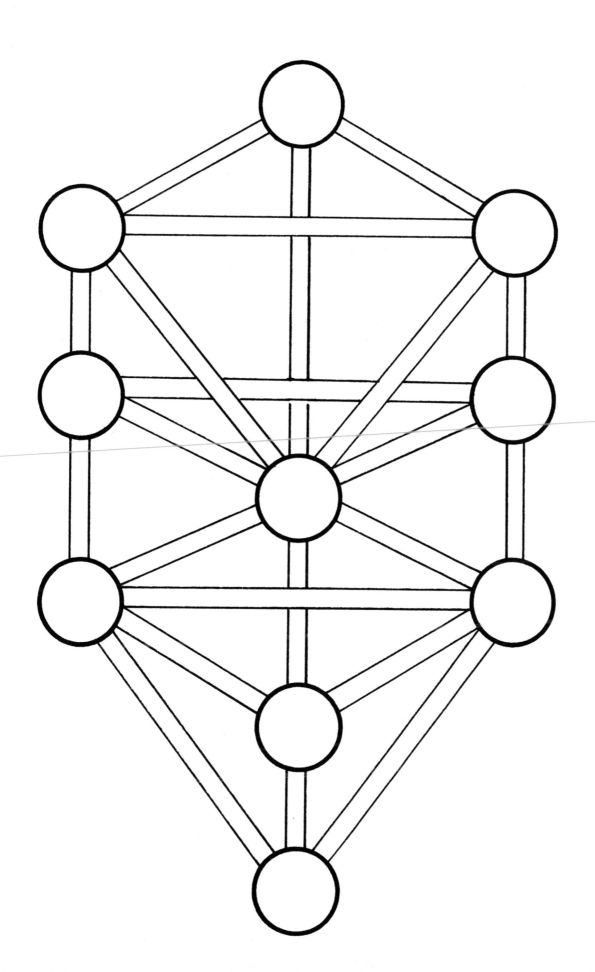

◆ THE WORLD OF FEAR AND SHADOW ◆

Among the journeys from the outside world of the geometrical patterns into the inside world with its secretive soul-patterns, the path of the Gypsies is probably the simplest one. Nothing prevents you from making yourself such a garden of self-consecration and beginning to travel. You should not feel pushed to do so, though. Listen into yourself and try to sense if you feel drawn in that direction. This is just one kind of meditation and maybe not yours at all.

According to my experience, you do not have to have fear at all. Whatever you will have to face can come only out of yourself. That, though, will be sometimes frightening and unpleasant. But in any case you will have to confront it at some time, and take the responsibility for it yourself. Since the thing you must face is here, after all, it is better—in my opinion—to know it and learn to accept it. In the long run this is even more pleasant than storing it always just in the subconscious, and then suddenly be forced to experience it unexpectedly, in that life which we think is the real one.

The question of the danger of the Mandala-meditation (but also any other effective meditation) can actually only be answered briefly: It is as dangerous as the Creation (because it is Creation that the Mandala represents); or somewhat more concretely, as dangerous as life, which ends with physical death; or even more concretely, as dangerous as the meditating persons themselves, because they will meet themselves at their worst or at their best.

In other words, you do not have to fear anyone but yourself. And if you have reason to be afraid of yourself, it is still better to look at your darkest shadow side than at some time to run up against it.

Since the Fall of Man, the human being is schizophrenic in his brain and also otherwise split. When psychiatry comes up with this diagnosis, it means the shadow half has gotten the best of it, or at least it very clearly asks leave to speak. The shadow does have a voice, and thank God one can hear that one, too. It might be good to listen to our own once in a while, before the psychiatrist has to do it (to whom it mostly does not tell much either).

The reference to possible danger should not discourage you. By voicing these dangers that you have known of for a long time, nothing changed—they were, after all, just as valid before. Only a very unconscious person can be scared by the reference to his having to die. Whenever the most banal facts still frighten us, we should simply meditate about how consciously we live at this point.

Stories about saints and realized masters from whichever tradition can explain to us that each minute of life is life-threatening—yes, in each second the "old Adam" could die.

The Indian Mandala on the opposite page is a Yantra, dedicated to the Goddess Kali; and thus it stands for the dark half of the Creation.

197

MANDALAS
IN THE WORLD
OF AMERICAN INDIANS

Turning to the traditional circle of the American Indians, we will not find Mandalas nearly as magnificent as the roses. Yes, the Native Americans did not even give their Mandalas lasting forms—if we disregard for now the teepees, their dwellings. But they have always consciously kept alive the Mandalas out of which grew their culture, or the Mandalas would have perished with the people. Even today, we have been only moderately successful in winning over the American Indians to white American cultural standards. Whenever they nevertheless have adopted our values, they forfeited many of their own. (Here one might ask if our own culture is not, after all, best for us.)

In order to be able to experience their sand-Mandalas, we have to familiarize ourselves with the foundations of these in the Indian life.

Bear in mind throughout this chapter that the American Indian traditions we speak of here were and are not common to all tribes in the nation and that, although many of these practices are still preserved in ceremony and ritual, they may or may not be a part of the everyday life of Native Americans today. Yet, on our path to the center, their traditions have much to teach all of us.

For the American Indian, creation is an expression of harmony, and he recognizes in it the law of polarity, like the law of the foursome resulting from it. Like all our ancestors, he recognized the dependence and the cooperation of the four elements and the four seasons, the four directions, the four periods of life, and the four human races. If one of the four poles got out of order, for the Native American the entire balance became mixed up. For example, since the four human races fought against one another, instead of complementing, nature with its four seasons had lost its rhythm and brought us catastrophes to remind us to turn back (also not an entirely new idea anymore).

The American Indian consciously tried to remain in harmony with nature and to learn from it. Thus he studied the minor and major events of his natural environment, and from that drew conclusions concerning the orderliness of the world. (In similar fashion, astrologers draw conclusions from the sky configurations and apply them to other levels.) He also applied this concept to himself. Thus the American Indian recognized his entire life story from external events with their signs. The inside was consciously tuned to the outside. Why should he keep secret something in the first place, when the Great Spirit knows—even before he does—everything that goes on in his heart.

The Native American also copied all his educational and training concepts from nature. Just as the young bird first is taken care of by the parents and is taught by the principle of imitation, in order then to be left on his own, so it also happened to the young Indian, who, in the ritual of puberty, suddenly found himself deserted and had to care for himself and had to take on responsibility. As the animals in their external camouflage colors, and also in their behavior, adapt to nature, also the Native American learned that from babyhood. But while he paid attention to nature, while he listened to it, he had to learn to become calm himself, to be able to silence his inner dialogue. American Indians also often together in company would keep silence. Just imagine that at a modern-day social event.

The Indian lived consciously with the rhythms of nature and was alert to the analogies of his life. Day and night were images of life and death to him. In the rise of the sun he experienced birth, and in the sunset, death. Sunrise and sunset were equally beautiful to him. In this respect, also in our culture there is a striking preference for these transition stages—because what is more often being photographed than sunsets? It is certainly an unconscious coming to terms with death, which we consciously shrink from.

The Native American has been a praying witness to the first appearance of the light; as well as to its farewell. Birth and death are equally welcome to him. Just as the night gives the soul access to other experiences, something similar happens after death. Each day thus reflects his life; each year in its seasonal rhythm lays down the pattern for Indian life. The strength of the sun during the four seasons

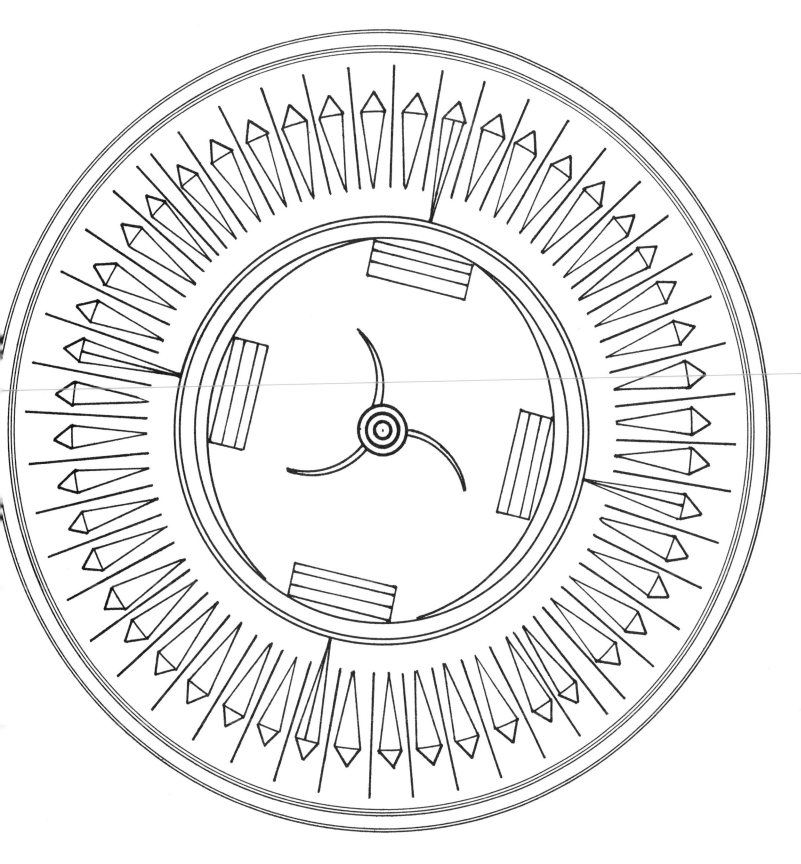

reflects for him exactly the strength in his four ages of life. Thus he has stood in the center of a Mandala consisting of many concentric circles, smaller and bigger ones, but all relate to one another and are an expression of the One center-point.

Many traditional actions of the American Indian's life show, in comparison to our present behavior, how far we have removed ourselves from our deepest needs. The new-born Indian baby was not torn out of its formerly harmonic, protected world (symbolized by a bubble-Mandala), with slaps on his naked behind, but the mother pressed her lips onto its mouth and this way inspired it with the first breath of life, very much the way our Biblical myth of Creation portrays it. The Native American child was not only allowed to remain longer in the harmonic center, also further on everything was done to lead it gently into its new life-circle. Whenever the rituals became not gentle and affectionate anymore, they were at least directly taken from nature. Thus the child always remained integrated.

Our children experience a childhood like that as an exception, though it is becoming more common in recent times to integrate and center our children as more and more we integrate and center ourselves. For us it is still something special not to torment the child at its birth, or to leave it with its mother. Calling these actions special betrays how far we had lost our way out of the center. On their own, the Indians might have never left it.

And as life begins differently, differently it ends. While in our "highly-civilized" culture the old people are being pushed aside and isolated, they were held in high honor among Native Americans, because for them old age was the time of wisdom, a time when one was not doing so much work in the world anymore, but when one, instead, came closer again to the center of the life-circle. Similar things hold true for death. It held nothing frightening at all, it was recognized as a natural transition into another stage of life of the soul.

In our culture we put forth every possible resistance to death. While the Native American totally consciously struck up his song of death or retreated to a deserted place to die, in order to be totally all-one again, we fight with all the devices of the world against what is, after all, unavoidable and necessary.

| Now paint a Native American Mandala of death.

200

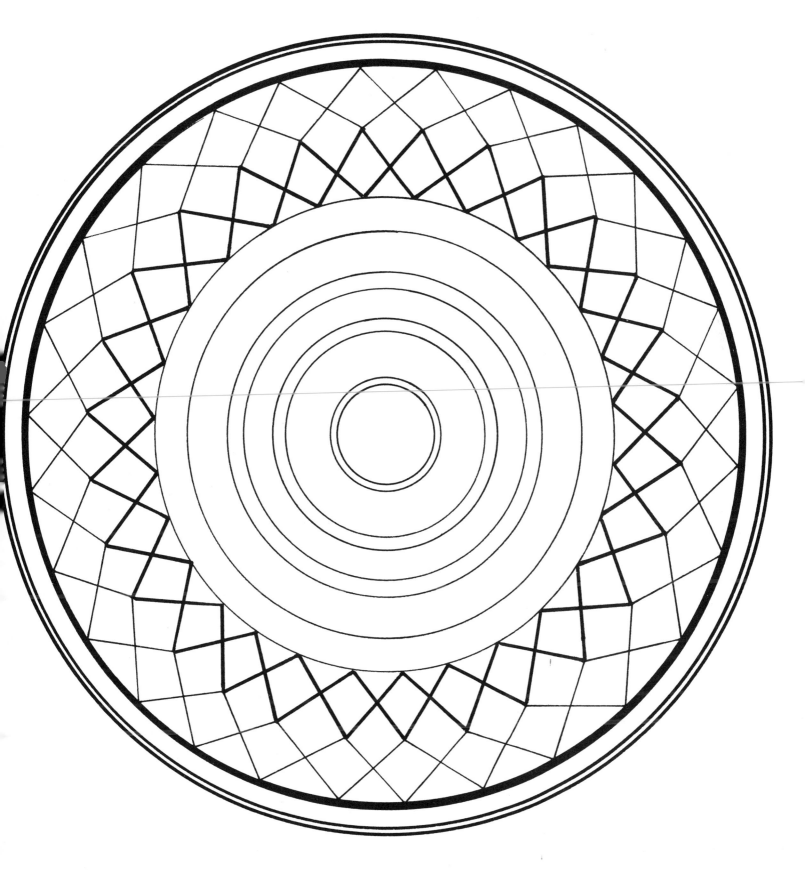

While Native Americans were concerned with the center of the Mandala, we stress its periphery and we are externally disappointed if the many, beautiful, colorful lights turn into the one white light again. It is the same rhythm that lets the flower develop from the seed and that leads back to the seed again. The American Indian accepted this rhythm and honored it. We, on the other hand, want to stop the whole cosmic game somewhere, for example at the flower, because we consider the flower to be especially beautiful.

This is the same attitude that would, when painting the Mandala, spare the center, because exactly there everything disappears again in the original point. That is also the attitude that wants to stop the wheel of fortune of the tenth tarot card somewhere at a spot which is comfortable for us (for our Ego)—for we want only fortune and thrust aside the misfortune, want only light and no shadow, only day and not night, want only to live and never to die.

Stopping the wheel is the surest way to cement the splitting of the consciousness to put us on the path into the duality—and thus into desperation.

The only alternative would be to *accept the unity of all things and, above all, of all pairs of contrast,* and to admit that there would not be day without night, there would not be any inhaling at all without exhaling, no prosperity without depression, no light without shadow, no peace without war, no white without black.

As almost all primitive races as well as highly developed cultures (Egyptians, Incas) have done, the American Indians prayed to the sun-Mandala, since they realized that the sun makes all life possible. In practically all cultures the orientation to the sun-rhythm was taught, and even in our time the sun still has enormous importance, for example, if we think about how much we let our life be determined by time. Any watch, even the most modern one, is, after all, a sundial and thus a Mandala.

Recently a colorful "anti-stress clock" has been available on our market, on which the time can be read only approximately. In the sun we have a much simpler, natural anti-stress clock. Maybe you will try at some point (e.g., during your next vacation) to act only according to this clock, and this way to find your connection again to the natural, inner clock, which all of nature follows.

◆ SUN COLOR CLOCK ◆

Reproduce the stages of the sun with colors in this simple twelve-part Mandala. On it place the sunrise, following the horoscope, on the left outside in the spot of the ascendant (that would be at 9 on the face of the clock) and the sunset opposite it at the spot of the descendant (3 on the clock). Take into consideration that well before sunrise and even long after sunset there is light and thus color in the sky.

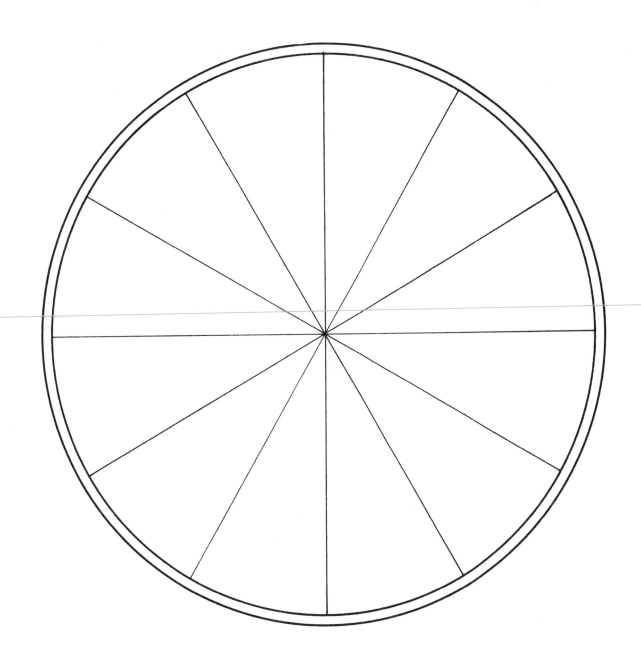

The adoration of the sun takes place even more distinctly in the rhythm of the year. Although we celebrate the solstice still without knowing it—as for example at Christmas—most people, nevertheless, take their vacation according to the sun. In upsurges of travelling, which in fact can be compared to the former mass migrations (those usually headed south), millions of people go on a pilgrimage towards the sun, sometimes creating for themselves considerable stress. Where the "adoration of the sun" takes place only on the most external level, one can burn in the process quite badly. The skin then lifts itself up in blisters (Mandalas) and bursts, and thus one opens oneself up completely.

Less painful, but more fulfilling, is the internal opening-up to the light. Generally one can state that the more material the chosen level is, the more combined with suffering is the redemption of practically all principles. This is still very familiar to us in simple examples: When one opens up in love to another person, this can lead into the seventh heaven; if one, on the other hand, opens up to sweets as a substitute for love, this will lead to grief-fat. This example, as already the sunburn showed us, applies to light and love. Unconsciously almost all people love the sun and open up to it with all their heart—but what else is love except opening oneself up, letting-in?

On the opposite page you see a Mandala dedicated to the Hindu Sun God, Surya.

Reverential towards the sun, the American Indians also revered the light of the night. Sun and moon were to them expressions of the polarity, and therefore equal in importance. They also show this basic dichotomy clearly in their Mandalas. There are two groups, Mandalas of the day and of the night. The ritual of the day began immediately after sunrise and had to be finished by sunset. In reverse, the ritual of the Mandala of the night began after sunset and ended again before its rise and thus its reputed extinction in its external form.

In all old cultures also, great importance was attributed to the moon-Mandala. Since it is the female aspect of the light, in our industrial cultures, dominated by male symbols, it has lost even more of its importance than the sun-Mandala. But all nations which, still bound to nature, live with the rhythm of the moon, make (for example) their plantings and harvests dependent on the phases of the moon.

Even in our culture, while we ignore most of nature's rhythms, the moon-rhythm, at least in its extreme points, is still felt.

Psychiatrists often experience that night shifts are very exhausting when the moon is full, since suddenly all patients "go crazy." But also sensitive people experience changes in their sleep, when the forces of the moon have a stronger effect. Gynecologists (whose task, after all, is the female, moonlike) know that during the full moon a lot more children are born; and that the 28-day cycle of a woman correlates exactly with the moon-cycle—and in the normal case is also coordinated in time. If in "modern" women the cycle frequently is irregular, that simply indicates that their rhythm is disturbed and that they are not in harmony with their natural environment anymore.

We also find today the devaluation of the moon as expression of the female part of the polarity (of the right brain) in our evaluation of "wonderful Sunday" and "ghastly Mo(on)nday." Probably our essential disregard of the moonlike night and its life has the greatest consequences for us. After all, we spend one-third of our lifetime in the unconscious empires of dreams and of unconscious sleep. And leaving psychotherapy out of account we ignore this third completely. So-called primitives again are the ones who show us that it is possible to make dreams a part of our lives—yes, to learn how to dream and even to wake up while in a dream.

Also for the Native American the dream-world played a crucial role. He paid close attention to it, and it strongly influenced his daily life. For certain developmental steps, for example, he first awaited his own dream suggestions. When you now begin to live with Mandalas, it is likely that this will also have effects on your dreams—you will increasingly meet Mandalas there.

In the psychology of Jung different cases of Mandala- and labyrinth-dreams are described; and we know that C. G. Jung considered dream-Mandalas as being healing factors in situations of crisis.

Now, we do not need to wait for crises to occur before opening ourselves up to these universal healing forces. The study of these patterns will activate you in the unconscious state, and thus also during the night. And Mandalas may appear not only in individual dreams—in the course of time you will discover that the dream-life itself corresponds to a Mandala, just as you could see it in the parallel of the Grail myth to "real life." All dreams group around a center, just as all events of life take place around a center.

THE WORLD OF RITUALS

We can experience something else very essential that is alive in Native American culture, something that lives an unloved, shadowy existence in our own culture, but nevertheless keeps us alive: the ritual.

The American Indians still use rituals, possibly more in ceremonies than in daily life. Rituals imitate life. That holds true in general for all rituals, whether we look at sacrifice ceremonies of the "heathens," Jews or Christians, or at the Mandala-ritual of Native Americans, or whatever. The life stemming from the ritual, out of the conscious experiencing or ritual imitating of analogies, does not lead us away from the circular course or interfere with the balancing forces of the environment.

Laws such as "action–reaction" correspond to "giving–taking"; both are the same, and were to the American Indian's living experiences. He knew, because he read it from nature, that for everything that he took he also had to give. Thus he did not take more than he needed at the moment and he did that with reverence. Here we have probably the explanation why some cultures have not experienced any progress in the polarized sense of the word.[1] They remained in the circular course in the Mandala, until we came and urged our mission onto them, influenced them, blackmailed them or with psychological finesse tried to pull them out of their circle.

Now, this is not the time and place for a sense of guilt, because that was, after all, "in the order," was even predicted by the prophets and saints of the cultures concerned—and these predictions were accepted. Here, too, the Mandala shows itself again: the path out of the center into the chaos and back. Entire nations experience the parable of the lost son: though everything may get lost in the outside, the internal knowledge about the one center is being preserved and finally leads back into it.

Since the American Indian on the one hand orientated his life strictly according to the rhythms given by nature, and on the other hand kept it flowing through his flexible life-style (no fixed house, hardly any personal belongings), he could also protect his rituals and Mandalas from the danger of torpor.

We are rather inclined to ignore natural rhythms, and in consequence have let our lives be turned into unconscious, even dead, rituals—because neither the Mandalas nor the rituals can be abolished completely. Thus we own the most magnificent Mandalas in the rose windows, but they remain empty shells, since there are hardly any people left who can bring them to life.

The Native American Mandalas, on the other hand, despite being extinguished in their external form after twelve hours at the latest, live on in the Indian who made them. The ceremony was being executed as "medicine," as consecration, and finally as healing and sanctification. Now, medicine was for the American Indian something completely different than for us—yes, almost the opposite. It reflected in his case the absolute faith in the Creation, in the Great Spirit—he surrendered to it. While the American Indian voluntarily retreated to die, we make attempts to revive.

The Native American lived in the circle oriented towards the middle. During the sand-Mandala ceremony, he ended up sitting exactly in the center of the circle and was celebrated in songs by the medicine man. Thus he became the center-point of the world, the altar, the deity. The medicine man, the one who was already ordained, transferred the Mandala onto the "patient" by placing his moistened hand onto the sand of the Mandala and then onto the body of the person sitting in the center. Thus the divine order was anchored in the "patient," and thus he also found the center in himself.

This bears a similarity to various group-therapeutic exercises, wherein one participant ends up in the middle and receives the energy of the whole Mandala in one form or another.

1. The film *Koyaanisquatsi* by Francis Ford Coppola illustrates this correlation in impressive images.

211

After the Mandala had been transferred to the human being, the medicine man took the sand and scattered the first part to the East, the next parts to the South, West and North. Finally he held up one portion to the Father in Heaven, and the last one he gave back to Mother Earth. What we already know from other traditions is here part of the ritual, of the dynamic Mandala. This form is so sacred to the Indians that they conduct it in an altered manner to protect the true ritual, when they demonstrate it to outsiders who are not in on the secret. They exchange directions, for example, whereby the right-turning magic circle, which correlates to the earth, becomes one turning to the left—which, after all, belongs to the counter-principle.

By that we can see how sensitive rituals and thus Mandala are, how easily they can be deprived of their sense and their original meaning—not so much through unconscious "mistakes" as through conscious intentions.

But because of that we do not have to be afraid we might draw the wrong Mandala. There is no wrong one and no right one, but only one that corresponds to the situation. If our own Mandalas always turn to the left, this is no reason to get uneasy; on the contrary, it is good to realize it. No one direction is better than another; there is no solution in any of them, because the solution lies in the center. Native Americans believed that each work of art and each ritual act was an expression and image of the Great Spirit. Thus each Mandala-ritual had its ceremonious setting and demanded a careful preparation: intensive cleansing, fasting, sweating, throwing up, sexual abstinence, solitary vigil. The American Indian expected, through that, to come in connection with an energy which used him to create the Mandala to consecrate and to heal.

Consciously or unconsciously behind all these preparations is the goal to become empty—in this emptiness/receptiveness can then be found the source to the one energy. Everything else falls off the body; only the essence remains, and it then creates the Mandala, which in turn reflects the essence in its core, in its center of strength. While the medicine man, because he was the consecrated one destined for the ritual, internally prepared for the ceremony, he looked on the outside for the necessary devices, such as sand, roots, and colors. He used only things which he found in his natural environment, and followed as much as possible the symbolism and analogy. If, for example, he was to perform a fertility-ritual he used a lot of yellow, the light shade of springtime; the material substance of yellow would be pollen, another fertility symbol.

Now, following the medicine man further through the ritual, we can observe one form of healing.

He begins with a period of strong concentration. All senses are being "caught" and directed towards a certain destination, i.e., the one goal, the one center. The alignment (orientation) of the senses is crucial in each ritual. Thus we find similar devices in all cultures. The vision of the Indian, for example, is centered on the forms and structures of the Mandala. The sense of hearing is directed by monotonous recitatives (chanting); sweet-smelling herbs of ritual significance are burnt in the sacred fire; and drugs that expand the consciousness may be employed. In addition to all this, the medicine man would execute strokes with an eagle's feather on certain areas of the patient's body; he then himself became the altar of the sacred act and therefore sat in the center. As in a therapeutic hypnosis, the patient fell into a trance, only that the medicine man did not use any suggestions. His devices to concentrate the consciousness onto one point were much more subtle, because they were completely in harmony with the natural environment of the Indian and in harmony with its cosmos.

Since Native Americans heard in everything always the One, the one divine melody, with these ceremonies they could treat animals, which they considered to be their brothers, and even influence nature (make rain).

Looking at other cultures, we find there astonishing concurrences. In our churches, especially once more in the domes and cathedrals of the Gothic, the worshipper's eye is caught by the pictures and colors of the windows, by the overwhelming depiction of the large roses, by the great high vaults. Chorales and invocations are sung, which in old days even more powerfully than today centered the spirit through their repetition. The entire structure of the Gothic cathedral lifts the spirit, directs the attention into the center of the church-cross where the altar stands, on which the transubstantiation‑takes place. By drinking wine and eating bread, this sacred transformation is brought even closer to each worshipper. Around the altar incense is burnt that envelops the sense of smell, and leads the spirit upwards with the smoke. In a different way, the upward-striving pointed arches do the same.

In rituals we are less familiar with, some of the devices may have been changed, depending on the culture—but the centration of the senses is always emphasized. So instead of incense sticks there may be scented candles or flower perfumes. The Indians chant Mantrams or listen to the chants of the Pandits reciting the Vedas; believers of the Eastern church follow the monotony of the heart-prayer, Catholics pray the rosary, and Muslims are centered in the order of their ornaments. All objects of the ritual and all rules are consistently in the service of the One, to draw the spirit to oneself and thus to let the transsubstantiation happen. The more concentric a ritual is, the closer it comes to the harmony of the cosmic Mandala, the better can the healing, the becoming whole, take place.

If we allow ourselves for once to really open our eyes, we will discover everywhere rituals that mark our seemingly so-rational life. And that is—just like everything that is— also in order, because we can never abolish the ritual, but at the most remove it, in the sense that we push it aside and then it ends up—like everything that is repressed—in the shadow. But the shadow exists in us just the same—only unconsciously—and at some point it will also obtain publicity and that way light.

So all of a sudden we develop compulsive acts—and what else is behind a compulsive desire to wash than a ritual of cleansing, which now, "completely incomprehensible" for the person afflicted and for his psychiatrist, struggles out of the depth and—thank God—cannot be suppressed anymore by anything medically.

But we do not even have to go to that extreme. Our society is full of rituals of compulsion. What is it, if one has to check twice that the door is locked? Once would be reasonably sufficient. What lies behind all the tics and small, senseless, but ever recurring motions? Luckily one can hardly rid oneself of these things. They are a necessary compensation for all the lost and forgotten rituals which were executed consciously. We have seen how, in principle, the religious rituals of different cultures are similar to one another, in that they aim at the same thing. Even in our modern time it is exactly these principles which alone are effective.

• EVERYTHING THAT HEALS IS RITUAL, OR IT DOES NOT HEAL •

That may seem very strange to you, especially expressed so pointedly—and to top it off, expressed by a doctor—but let's have a look at ourselves in this respect. Just as the American Indian fell sick along with his natural environment and was healed by its devices and symbols, so are we, who fall sick with our technological, rationalized, and emotionally cold environment, being treated in our own health-factories. But hands are seldom laid on us anymore, because we also learned not to touch each other!

So far everything fits together, and there is not the slightest reason to fight our modern medicine; there is no reason to fight anything. The principle of homeopathy (to heal the same with the same) has been preserved and is growing more popular, and the ritual is in order.

If we change, our medicine will change also, paralleling our change. Every one of us finds his equivalent, just as each Native American searches for his medicine and finds it in tradition. And even if some other tradition seems ever so different to us, it is not, because the principle in effect remains the same: the ritual.

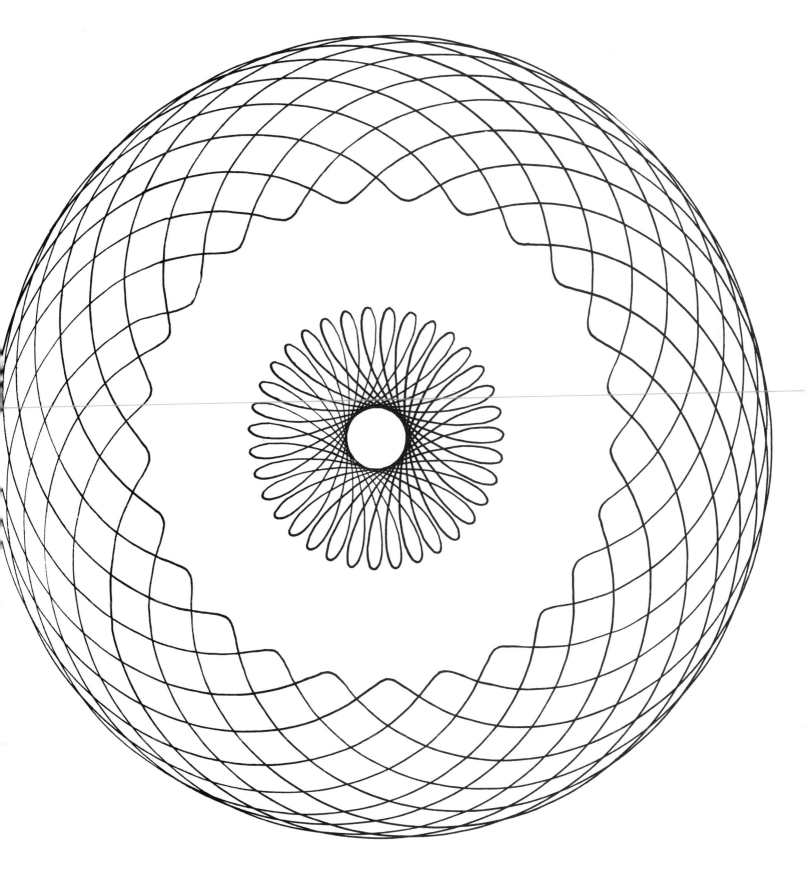

◆ A MODERN HEALING-RITUAL ◆

You flash back to that situation when you last visited a doctor. With slight excitement you enter his waiting room. Immediately you are surrounded by a peculiar, special smell of "medicine." You announce yourself to a woman clad all in white and then you have to wait for the time being, until **it** happens, until you enter **his** presence. While waiting, you usually sit in a **circle** with other, similarly expectant patients. For an entire hour you pay close attention to the succession of patients being called in, because, after all, you want to see him as soon as possible. Then the moment arrives. The woman clad in white fetches you out of the large circle, because now it is your turn.

She takes you with her to the smallest but most important room which, as a sign of its importance, is filled with strange equipment and objects, of which you know little or nothing at all. Here **it** happens—you are in **his** presence. He too is clad in bright white. You have no choice but to entrust yourself to him completely, to tell him everything openly and to simply surrender yourself. He handles the strange equipment and objects skillfully and knowingly. And you were right: He understands you, knows immediately what is wrong with you, and as proof of that he takes out a pen and draws on a small piece of white paper (at lightning speed and with dreamlike confidence) some signs, the importance of which you do not have the slightest idea of, but which are, all of them, just there for you. This way you now have your "medicine."

Although you cannot read the magic characters of your doctor, that other magician, again clad in white, the pharmacist to whom you go next, can read it, and in exchange for your paper he will give you a small, secretive vial, on which is written a series of syllables which again does not tell you anything. When you swallow the small wonderpills at home, although you do not taste much, you feel nevertheless immediately that "something" is happening. You feel at once much more relaxed; the pinching and twinging in your body hardly bothers you anymore. With the help of the right "medicine" you can get rid of all these trifles, and you become more and more convinced that "everything is in order," because you feel understood and accepted by **your** medicine man. And in case at some point something else gets out of order, you just go back to him, and he then restores that to order.

Everything that works is ritual, and so this scene was not presented out of a desire to make fun of it. Quite on the contrary, this is an attempt to turn again consciously to the ritual. It is just as much in order to seek healing in a church as in a doctor's practice or in a sand-Mandala ritual.

As long as the ritual still functions, in fact, everything is in order. Much more "dangerous" is the attempt to see through the rituals to intellectualize them, in order to abolish them . . . because one is so reasonable and enlightened. If the medicine of today ever dispenses with the pharmacist, it will soon be standing empty-handed in front of its patients. For those who still believe in the scientifically exact effects of our medicine, we will remind you that science—smart as it undoubtedly is—will eventually find itself out, as when so-called "placebo experiments" showed that the effect of many psycho-pharmaceutical drugs is rather identical to the placebo effect. Unknown to the patient, placebos do not contain any "chemical medicine" at all.

I do not want to cast doubt on the effectiveness of the medical drugs in general, except that they have nothing to do with healing. Just in case you strongly believe in chemomedicine, stick to it. Maybe it is your last belief, and it is still effective—for it is clad in a ritual. Furthermore, this ritual also applies to the practice of medicine. (Let us think, for a moment, of the ritual which is behind a lawsuit.)

Luckily for us, so far as we can see, we have not succeeded in abolishing rituals completely. Wherever we look, we will always rediscover them, if we are only open to the idea. Today we must look closer, because the rituals are more subtle, hidden in the area of the shadow, while they were formerly celebrated openly in the cathedrals.

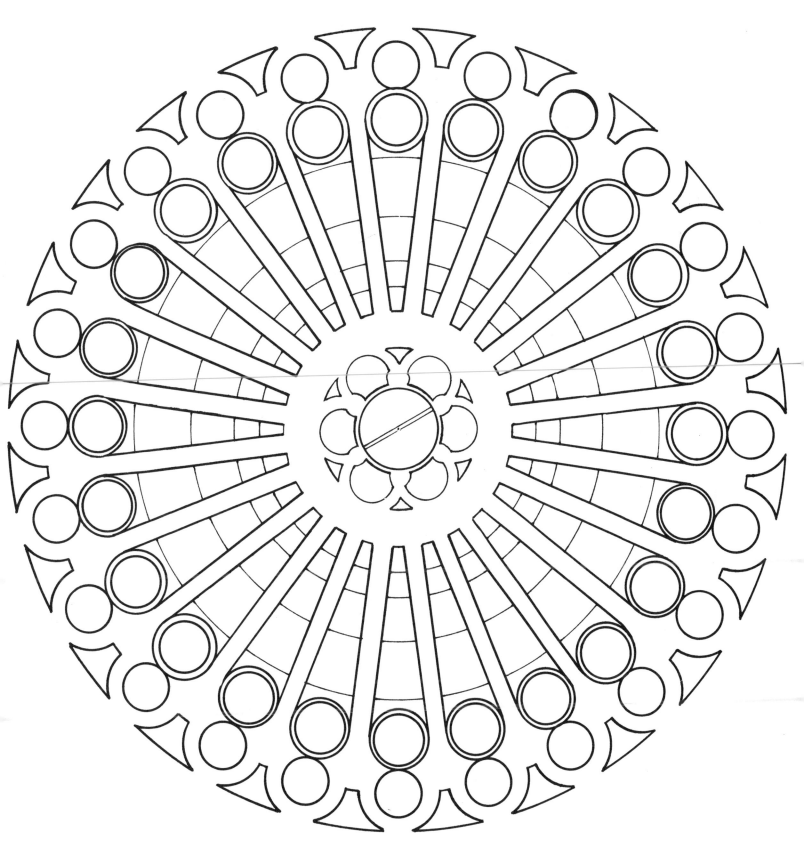

We draw one last truth from the ritual of the American Indians: They are not concerned with the individuality, with the Ego of the person performing the ritual. Often the faces are even concealed, behind masks. It is not the medicine man who heals, but a greater power that heals through him. He becomes tool of the One, because he can free himself from his Ego or because he allowed himself to become "pure being"—empty. In this emptiness the One can be effective, and the Indian trusts in the knowledge that the One knows better what has to happen than he himself with his small, restricted horizon.

He trusts the large circle:

"Your will be done!"

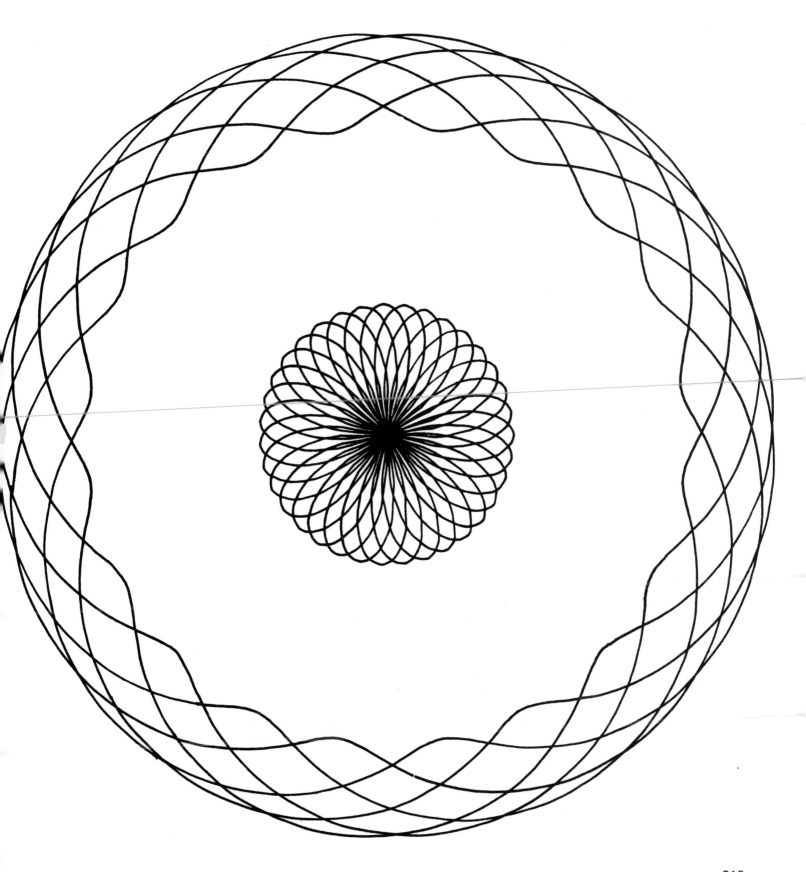

◆ LEVELS OF ENERGY ◆

For us to adopt the historic rituals of old civilized nations and those of the American Indians would be very difficult, and probably does not even make sense, because we would not be able to achieve anything better than more or less embarrassing imitations. On the other hand, trying them can help us a lot in recognizing the general principles of the ritual, so that we find the path to the rituals and Mandalas that fit into our time and environment, and that open us up again to our center.

In this center lies everything and nothing, depending on our point of view. In it we can experience that unimaginable strength and energy which holds the microcosm human being together. The closer we get to the center-point, the more powerful becomes the force.

This phenomenon, at which we now want to have a closer look, has its parallel in the macrocosm. When we occupy ourselves with Mandalas, we will get a feeling for those great energies with which we deal. Also in the macrocosm, as we go deeper, the power and energy become greater and the levels become finer.

A good example is war, "the father of all things," as Heraclitus formulates it. From destruction we can learn a lot about energies. We begin at a very elementary level, and punch an "enemy's" face with our fist. Our action becomes a little more subtle and more effective when in addition we use physical science and shoot a small lead bullet into his stomach. The next step becomes even more effective, on the even finer level of chemistry, when we use poison. On that same level, getting more refined because we are already working with molecules, is poison gas or even biological poison—gas made out of viruses. If we go even further to the atom and also penetrate into its nucleus—then we have reached nuclear fission and thus the atomic bomb. With each step our actions become less and less obtrusive, yet more and more deadly.

Probably everybody can remember a comparable experience when one did a lot more harm with a single word than he might have done with a blow of the fist. Looked at in this way, we can work with the Mandala on any energy level, depending on how much we yield to its tendency to draw us towards the center.

Energy is value-free, neither good nor bad, nor just as good as bad. All the way in the center this comparison stops anyway. There everything is energy, and it is valueless, in the same way that that internal light of the center is colorless and nevertheless contains all colors.

Now create your own ritual out of the depth of your fantasy, in order to apply it to your next Mandala. Maybe for a change you will also work with the idea of the American Indians: that the Mandala portrays you, and you portray yourself in it.

Here are some hints that can help, but may impede you if you follow them slavishly:

1. Preparation: We find a very basic and effective form of preparation for the rituals in the culture of the Essenes or also of the Navajo Indians, who at completely different times and in completely different places on earth prepared themselves very similarly for important ceremonies. In order for the external, the sand-Mandala, to be pure, and to reflect the pure order clearly, first one's own internal Mandala is cleansed through fasting. In addition, through fasting, the senses, including the sixth sense, are being sharpened, so that the sensitivity increases for visions and unusually vivid mental images.
2. Orientation (in space, in time)
3. Visual tuning-in (candles, flowers . . .)
4. Acoustic tuning-in (music, Mantrams)
5. Tuning-in of the sense of smell (oils, scented candles, scent-sticks, incense . . .)
6. Clothing (you can wear to your ritual clothing that envelops you, impedes you, caresses you . . .)
7. You can dedicate the Mandala to an event or a person (or to yourself)
8. You can orientate your consciousness onto the **one** center.

If you should actually enter a ritual, you will soon realize that "it" will work and happen all by itself, because, after all, we are really not that far away from the center. In order to become calm in a cathedral, one does not need to be a priest. Whoever learns to plunge completely into a Mandala ritual will find total calmness in its depth without having to do anything consciously.

The next Mandala was drawn with the compass only and consists throughout of Mandalas.

MANDALA GAMES

This book should be more play than book, I said at the beginning; and so now we want to dedicate ourselves completely to playing with the Mandala. Being itself an image of cosmic play, it is of course excellently suited for play (in the sense that children do it) but also for "learning" again how to play as adults. In this connection "learn" may be misleading, since we usually associate stress with learning.

In this sense it would be more accurate to say it can help, in a playful way, to recover the ability to play. We can also use as a model the childlike unconcern about making mistakes. "Mistakes" are always opportunities, since they show us what we don't know. Each mistake can be made

into something, can be further developed—then it just becomes something other than what we had planned—so what? More play and fun can develop out of a mistake or a coincidence than out of any seriousness.

Also this book, in the last analysis, developed out of a mistake: i.e., out of my ocular shortsightedness and preoccupation with optic vision and the viewpoint that came of that. Thus also the soft look is a "natural mistake" of many nearsighted people. Above all, in this book I am preoccupied with what I want to learn myself. The idea for this book and the Mandala patterns, for example, emerged on a journey to French and Spanish cathedrals.

♦ MEDITATION IN A CATHEDRAL ♦

When you enter a cathedral the next time, try, for a change, the soft, relaxed way of looking. Sit upright and in a spot where you can comfortably look at a rose. Then you widen your horizon beyond the rose, until you experience the nave in its totality—freed from all details, which, after all, have value only as contribution to the harmony of the whole. Through the slight fuzziness of the unfocused vision, the looked-at becomes blurred; everything becomes equally important—of the same value—and thus becomes un-valued. But to the same degree that the valuation disappears, also the intellect calms down, since where there is

nothing to value and to evaluate, the intellect is simply out of work and relaxes as well. Neither eyes nor ears nor any other sense furnishes it with concrete material. Probably it will try for a while to occupy itself with old remembered details. But also it will be calm at some time and meditation can begin.

Now try to create the rose of the Cathedral of St. Étienne at Châlons-sur-Marne softly, right from the beginning:
a) with soft colors
b) with soft borders
c) or however

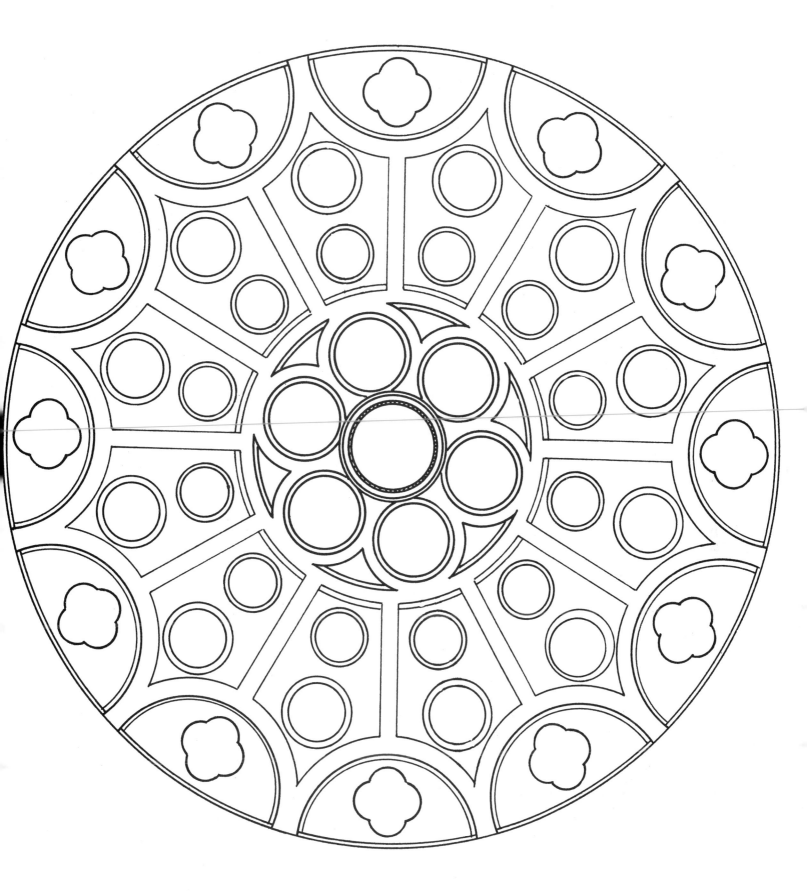

Now we want to switch off the external light for some time and open ourselves to the internal one. To do that, sit down comfortably upright, close your eyes and place both palms over them, so that with your forefingers you can exert a certain pressure on the eyelids and thus on the eyeballs. Then you experience that there is no darkness in them at all; instead you see the most varying patterns and light perceptions, including the Mandala. Do this exercise first, and take your time at it, just as for everything else.

This way it is even possible to experience a living image of your own retina, similar to the way you previously experienced the painted one, only this time in living colors.

Do this exercise as often as you wish, and discover through it that in front of your internal eye there is about the same amount of activity, whether you look to the outside or to the inside—an experience that every person has when he/she dreams at night with closed eyes.

Always, when we try to place blame on something in the outside, we are unaware of the fact that everything also has to be inside. So this simple exercise can help us to awake and to open up our internal eyes—and to take on ourselves the responsibility for us and for our environment. But no meditation technique can open us up more than our own internal world, our own Mandala.

If you feel like it, of course you can have similar experiences with the other senses; for example, by closing the external ears in favor of the internal ones and devoting yourself to your internal sounds. Or you close up your nose or even mouth, and listen to the internal monologues that go on despite that. This last exercise, though, is less fun, simply because we play that game day in day out and at night as well.

As little as we keep our external mouth shut, we never keep the internal one shut. But that is the goal of all meditation techniques, like Mantram meditations, concentration exercises, Zen, etc. It is what Don Juan, the American Indian teacher of Carlos Castañeda, would relate to the stilling of the internal monologue. Certainly it is an impressive experience to listen, for once totally unconsciously, to this perpetual stream of thought which constantly flows in us. Try also to bring it to a halt—just for a minute. It sounds so simple, but nevertheless we cannot do it.

Repeat this exercise as often as you like. Often these techniques may be combined, by closing eyes, ears, and mouth at the same time. Pick an exercise you prefer, then do it more often, maybe even regularly. Then you will realize, though, that your intellect suddenly objects to it, because with regularity the exercise becomes dangerous for the intellect, and it will not rest until it convinces you (of course for good reasons, because they are its specialty) that you should do the exercises less often. Even if you begin to see through the intention of the intellect, do not be mad at it. This is its only, and maybe its last, chance. Just watch it at its game. If you do that long enough, you will suddenly realize that there is a difference between your intellect and you. This initially slight suspicion can bring you into the middle between right and left. But somewhere there has to be also the land of enlightenment.

On the opposite page you see the Castel Sant'Angelo in Rome.

So far you will have painted most of the Mandalas from the center towards the outside. This corresponds with the coming into existence of the Creation, the exhaling of Brahma, or our own development throughout time. Now, for a change, consciously take the reverse path: from the periphery to the inside, the unmaking of the Creation, Brahma's inhaling and your own way home.

Pay attention to the fact that this Mandala emerges almost solely from straight lines. Also pay attention to the fact that all tips (>) that emanate from the center also form tips inwards. Every aggression that turns to the outside at the same time also turns to the inside.

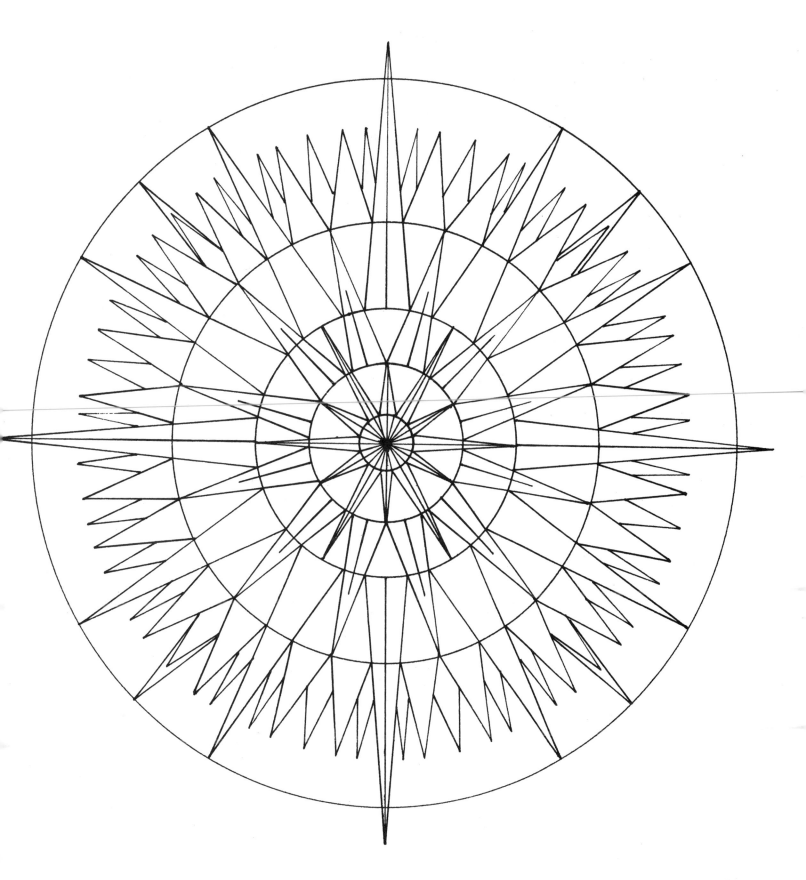

Now repeat the same exercise as a constructive exercise. So far, since it makes sense, you have designed all Mandalas starting with the center-point. When you go the reverse way, constructing from the periphery inwards, you will realize how difficult it is to start with the way back, before one has travelled the way that leads there. On another level this would correspond to the attempt to let go of the Ego before one has gotten to know it.

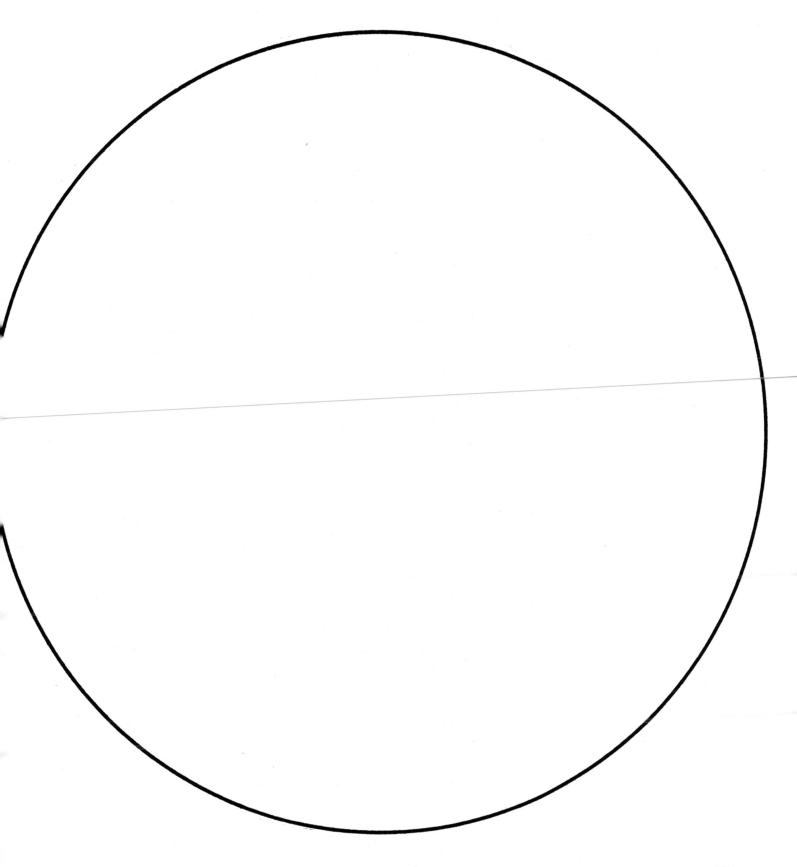

You can also use the Mandala as measurement, measurement in a rather nonmaterial sense—neither as space- nor as weight-measurement, nor as real time-measurement—but best as development-measurement. For example, if you do a Mandala before and after an important, drastic experience (before and after a world trip, therapy, etc.), see what changes in you.

This principle can be extended at pleasure. You can start a diary in the form of a Mandala: one for each day, or for each week, each month. You can also create the week-Mandala in such a way that you construe yourself as one with seven layers and each day you paint one.

On the opposite page you see a Mandala made almost entirely of soft heart-shapes.

When you want to do Mandala rituals, the orientation is an important prerequisite. Now, one can not only orientate oneself in regard to space, but also in regard to time. Rituals, after all, always took place at special moments of time or during special events, like the Equinox, or moments in life that are especially urgent. We can create rituals to suit any special occasion.

Let us also think of the horoscope, in which for us one special moment will be found, because it distinguishes itself through a particularly high quality of time. At such a point we could just as well execute a ritual with a Mandala meditation, or with the creation of a Mandala, and afterwards contemplate ritual and Mandala and interpret them.

But it is not the meaning and goal of this book to assist in interpreting or to even offer an introduction to the divinatory possibilities of the Mandala. In general, one can use any system to interpret, if one knows the system, and thus, of course, this is possible with Mandalas. Knowledge and intuition in this direction grow most quickly and directly from intensive study of the Mandalas of one's own birthday, of the New Year, or of any other beginning. Or you might make a Mandala for somebody for his/her birthday. You cannot give a more personal gift than yourself.

The Mandala on the opposite page stems from a Portuguese banknote.

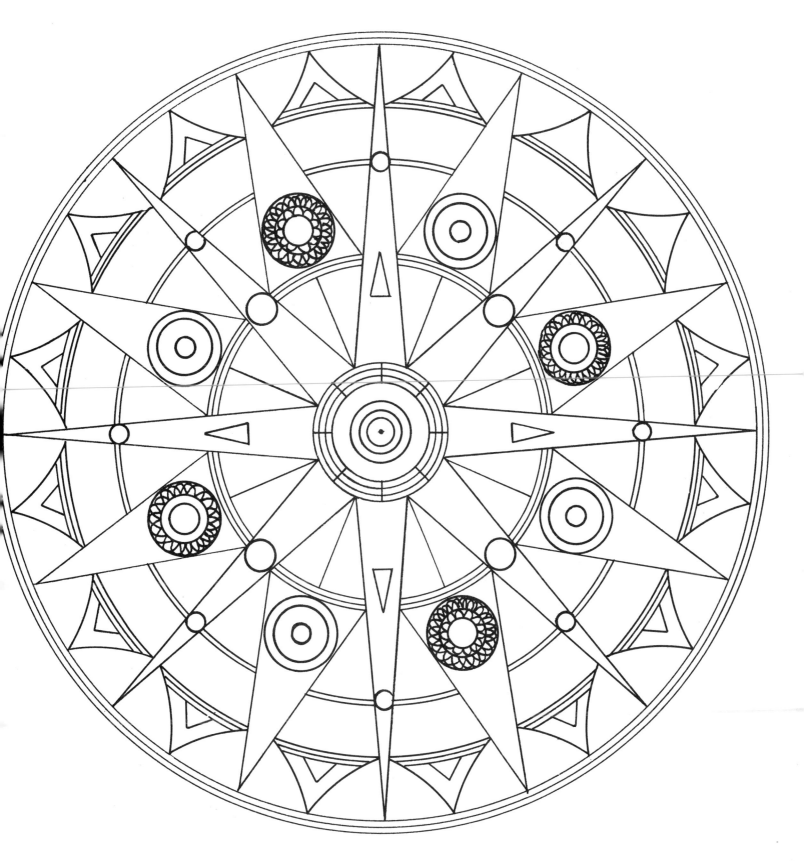

The game can also become exciting, even suspenseful, with colors. Choose colors blindly: close your eyes and pick the next color out of the heaps of your colored pencils and execute the next level of Mandala with it (attention! the intellect with its tricks especially likes to take part in this). This procedure is especially suited for Mandalas of certain events, since the unconscious can play along even more clearly.

Using rational color choice, the reverse of the last exercise, you choose the colors consciously—e.g., in rainbow succession: (infrared)—red—orange—yellow—green—blue—violet—(ultraviolet) (see Glossary, *rainbow*). The terms in parentheses show you that the spectrum does not stop there where our capability to see stops. If you can imagine playing this Mandala game with a bat, you would be surprised; the bat, you must know, sees totally different color frequencies.

Another possibility lies in limiting the colors. For example, use only two colors in constant alternation; or complementary colors alternately; or, with the Mandala of the weekdays, the color of the respective day in each layer; etc.

If you know your horoscope, you can create it as Mandala: the houses in colors that correlate with them, the planets in their respective colors with their radiations. Pay attention to the fact that here in the center stands the planet earth, and the even more exact center is the point on the Mandala earth were right now you are being born. You can depict the aspects as colorful energy-connections—which you are as well.

The horoscope offers the most varied play possibilities. You can, for example, place on your individual horoscope the original pattern of the labyrinth of Chartres. You place the entrance of the labyrinth onto the ascendant, and see what develops from there. . . . Possibly, from the combination of two patterns, a third one, that makes sense, emerges . . .

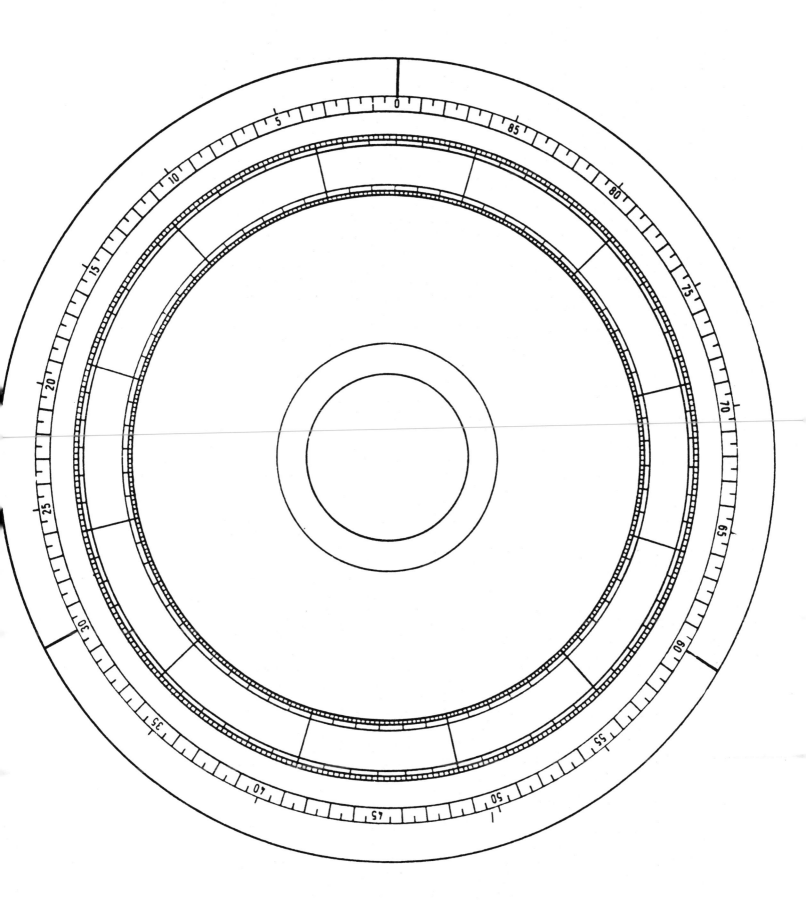

Each path through a Mandala can be a symbolic pilgrimage—pay attention to what happens when you travel while painting. . . .

When you have finished, you meditate about the journey. With a composed look (without blinking!) contemplate your Mandala and wait until it starts to move.

Try it. The colors and structures come alive after a while. (You do not have to believe in it beforehand—only you are not allowed to disbelieve it. If you do so, then you will be right, for "your" Mandala will then not come alive).

Experimenting with different materials:

Use felt-tipped pens or colored pencils, crayons, water colors, dirt, acrylic paints, oil paints; it can also be fun to mix different materials! Some paints, like felt-tipped pens or acrylic, because of their brilliant quality, are especially suited for Mandalas as bases for optic journeys. Or you may use watercolors and watercolor paper, which you wet—this way you can create very soft Mandalas. Especially when you are doing "partner-Mandalas," this technique can result in exciting mixtures and differences.

You can dedicate your Mandalas to certain themes or theme cycles: a Mandala for each season, one for each element (fire, water, air, earth), a Mandala for each member of the family, etc. . .

The Mandala of the earth . . . real or with the colors that you want to give the individual parts of the earth or the countries . . .

On the opposite page is another Mandala that consists only of circles.

In case emotions rise up while you are playing, this is, of course, all right. Each Mandala is like a tree—to the external, visible part relates a corresponding invisible one, which is there whether or not we see it. We always see just the one half of the polarity, but still have to live with both of them. Think about our eye exercises. We cannot see much more than half the circle, even with the broadest field of vision, and so the other half remains in the shadow—not visible to us, but still always present. Therefore have regard for yourself and for your shadow, and be happy when it occasionally emerges; it is there anyway.

By the way, this is not the newest psychological knowledge, but very old knowledge of long-gone cultures. So it was always the goal of the American Indians to hold the head high up in the clouds and to be rooted with the legs deeply in Mother Earth. All our ancestors knew about the shadow half. They built their churches with a light, visible part and a hidden, subterranean one, the crypt. In Chartres this principle was especially followed. The entire cathedral corresponds in its measurements to harmonic laws: its vault is 37 meters (40 feet) high above the earth, and exactly as deep underneath the earth lies the water level of the old Celtic fountain in the consecration cave, on top of which the cathedral was built.[1] Maybe this will encourage you to stand by your own traditions.

---

1. Compare L. Charpentier. *The Secret of the Cathedral of Chartres.* Cologne: Gaia, 1972.

A Mandala which is especially suited to entice emotions to come out of their depth is one in which you place five original forms or Indian Tattwas (square, half-moon, triangle, circle, and point) into harmonic connection to each other in a Mandala.

The rise of the emotions becomes even more distinct if you go into the third dimension and reshape such original forms (for example, with Plasticine or clay) in their exact forms. In the space we then deal accordingly with square, half-moon, pyramid, and globe. Point remains point. These original forms activate the original forms in us, and we then feel them within ourselves. With this exercise it is especially difficult to find the invisible center that is the basis of the symmetry of our own three-dimensional creation. We cannot see this center, we can only let it come into existence through its external form. Whenever we do not succeed in doing so, it may bring about appropriate emotions.

The resolution to make a Mandala, for a change, with the left hand can also evoke deep feelings. "I can do it with my left hand" means, after all, to do it lightly, without much deliberation, smoothly and without difficulty. But that exactly corresponds to our neuroanatomic realizations about the brain, because it is just the right half of the brain that dominates the left hand.

In a very simple way this exercise demonstrates how difficult it has become for us right-handed people, who think analytically, to do something with the left. Therefore paint the next Mandala very consciously with your left hand—should you be left-handed, switch to the right hand. It is a question of the fifth, or larynx Chakra. The original colors are:

    blue-grey for the lotus petals,

    silver for the half-moon,

    white for the circle and the central triangle.

The remaining associations and also the form-elements change.

In case you should get bored on vacation at the beach, you can create sand-Mandalas—and you can sit down in their middle and meditate. (If you play your cards well, you can, by doing so, easily become the "guru" of other bored tourists.) Or you draw the labyrinth into the sand and then consciously follow it; or design new mazes for yourself or for whomever you wish.

With the labyrinth you can do many painting color games. As archetypical image of the path, it is especially suited for realizing the function of doubt and criticism on the path.

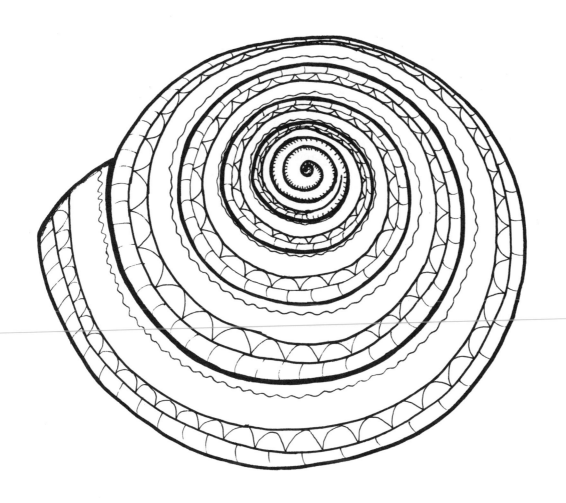

In case you have a flair for exact drawings, you can tackle a rose window and recreate it on a large scale and with all its figurative images. People who are good at handicraft can transform the rose-Mandalas back into light-images. If it is clear to you that all stone structures appear to be black when the light is shining in one's eye (like the examples on pages 86 and 87), so you can glue colorful foils onto black poster board, and when the light shines on it you will have a luminous Mandala. Especially suited for that purpose may be the flame-roses of the Late Gothic (here is the one of Beauvais).

The next, more graphic exercise concerns the wheel of life. Paint it with its twelve spokes and draw individual important episodes of your life onto the one (ascending) or other (descending) side. You can also portray the episodes and events in symbols. When you have finished, make yourself aware that each event on the descending branch is followed by an ascending event and vice versa, and hereafter take notice of the fact that no law of causation is dominating, but solely the law of balance.

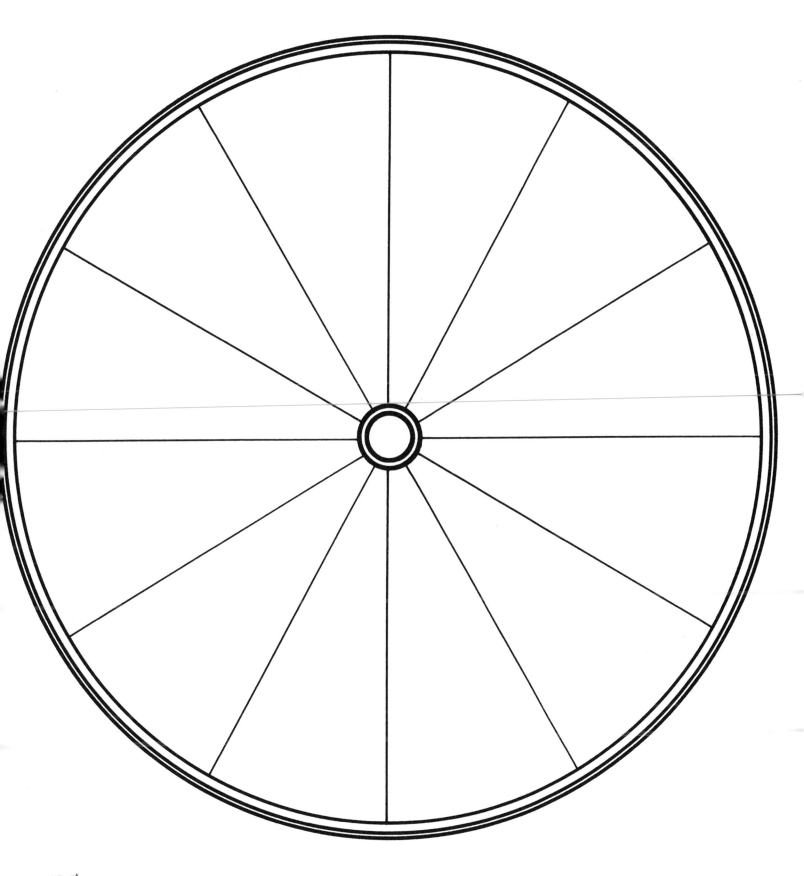

Create a very large Mandala of the universe in the shape of the Taoistic T'ai Chi. Do it as large as you dare, maybe even a bit larger.

Now experience, while painting, how therein again and again smaller new worlds are created, which maybe all consider their world to be the only one, or at least the most important one, up to the world of the most fleeting and, if you wish, even further . . .

And then you make yourself aware of the fact that your large Mandala is only the one point of the next larger one . . .

Possibly you consider this game still too childish for you, or maybe you only participate "for the sake of others." Bear in mind that it is quite a lot to do something for the sake of other people.

If instead you'd rather know more about Mandalas, you will find here further literary references.

But bear in mind: Who experiences the music? The music critic, who reads the full score as the music is playing and who wants to inform himself, or the one who "only" enjoys the music, or even the musician? Who gets more from an apple? The child who takes a bite of it or the biochemist who analyzes it?

You do not have to put yourself onto the play level; maybe instead you have a circle of friends, you can sit together, drink together, listen to music or do something—have conversations or discussions or disputes or whatever. And in doing that, you do a Mandala-ritual—unconsciously, but nevertheless. Also in your circle is a middle, and it is empty or contains a symbol such as a fire or nourishment. The spiritual nourishment in any case comes out of the center, and this Mandala-ritual is really common to all human beings—it is universal.

It is possible, though, that the Mandala-ritual evokes dark and heretofore unconscious forces, but it can of course bring about happiness, pleasure, satisfaction, and other emotions that we like. In the end it can even connect us with that source of unlimited energy within us—that source out of which everything comes into existence and into which everything has to go back again. There lies an unlimited potential of healing and becoming whole.

Now that we are on the way there, we experience the early effects of this unlimited energy source; we can meet our own inner doctor, which is far superior to all the outside doctors; we can also rediscover our intuition.

The way there is really not far; it has no expansion in space and time at all—the source is always there already. Chaos and cosmos always exist at the same time, they penetrate each other, and which aspect we perceive at any given time depends only on the visual angle. To live consciously out of the Mandala means to experience always—amidst all the chaos of this polar world—the order of the unity as well.

In our own way we generally tend to divide chaos and cosmos: we see the chaos on the outside, especially in others, and the cosmos, the order, we see in ourselves. Also that is a game, and it is almost the most fun of all. So it is difficult to find other games, which convey only approximately as much fun and satisfaction. But as soon as we have realized that we always project everything only out of ourselves, we can play this projection game consciously. And we do not even have to take back the projections.

We paint the Mandala of our partner's hate onto ourselves, or the rage of the neighbor onto ourselves, or the inadequacy of our father (of our mother), or of the hopelessness of the whole situation. In case we realize from this that these feelings are also ours, that does no harm. Theoretically we have long known this. And this way you can also paint the Mandala of your sorrow, your sympathy, your pleasure, or your love.

It is now time to release oneself little by little from the situations and limits of this book, to release oneself from its pattern. Probably you have already realized that Mandalas are really everywhere; now suddenly they jump into your eye wherever you look. Thus you can, of course, create Mandalas out of everything and everywhere, out of river pebbles as well as out of colorful fall foliage, out of flowers and petals, as well as out of fruit bowls and cores. You can set the table as a Mandala, garnish the food on your table as such, you can rediscover the Mandala in each roll and in the cakes. On the trail of Native Americans, Mandalas can be created out of grass and other parts of plants, out of fir needles, pine cones, and bird feathers. Or it could just as well be a kitchen-Mandala: made out of grains or other seeds, spices or waste . . . (each peel of an apple that is peeled off in one piece makes a spiral and this way is a Mandala).

There is no limit to your fantasy. Fabric and fur leftovers are suited just as well as shells or screws.

Each walk, each trip can turn into a Mandala, if you collect materials for it on the way and finally arrange them together into a picture. Maybe just by doing that you will find out what it was that you were circling.

With sand at the ocean, or clay or Plasticine, you can even conquer the third dimension. Maybe you also experience your house, your city, your country as Mandalas, as stations on the way to the Mandala earth.

Maybe you have already realized that many of these exercises are also suitable for games to be played in twos or in a group. Here are some suggestions especially for partner or group games.

It is the point of the most simple partner game that each of you alternately chooses a color and paints a layer. That alone creates a strange dependency on each other. Pay attention to how you feel in that case—whether you tend to violate the limits or whether you do not even dare to come close to your limit; whether you let your partner paint or whether you must comment on his painting, must interfere and go so far as to meddle with it or even paint over it.

This way once in a while you can play a "game of Mandala"—special moments are of course especially suited.

This can be brought one step further, when each of you chooses the color for your partner and vice versa. So he/she has to execute your work and you his/hers. Once you can do this without conflict, meditate about the question of whether you have possibly already gotten used to leading your life differently—or is it really your flexibility that complies with everything?

Or have you simply begun already to *play*?

267

An exciting picture can be created if you divide the Mandala on the diagonal and each of you paints one half. Do your two halves together actually make a whole? You might divide the Mandala with a line, or you can simply cut it. If you cannot see what your partner is doing on his half, do the two halves then still fit together? Or do they fit especially well, now that you are more open?

It makes sense to do this last exercise alone, because in each of us live two beings, after all. This way you can unite your two polar soul-parts (the female and the male) in one Mandala.

In a group it is always worthwhile to play a game (for example, paint a layer alternately) with the member of the group whom you like least, to start out just with him/her on the way to the unity (i.e., from the outside to the inside).

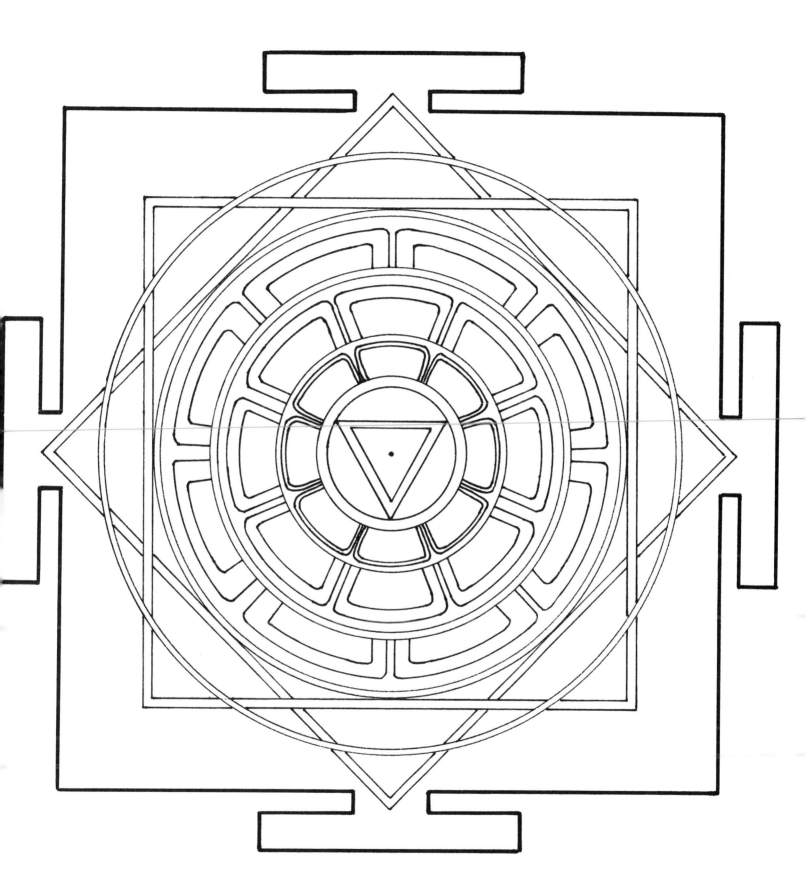

Then you repeat the same thing with the group member you like best and experience how much you really are at one with each other. These games have a special appeal if you hold your tongue and really pay attention to **yourself.**

When you talk, the whole thing often turns into group dynamics, which can also have its appeal. If you do not get to paint anymore at all, you simply have to rename the game. In that case, though, you will end up very quickly with your favorite games that you have known all along. If you play some kind of group games for which you have to pick a partner from your group, you choose, for a change, according to the Mandala. That may be more honest than choosing according to the face, and more exciting.

On the opposite page you see an Assyrian Mandala.

Each partner or group game becomes more intensive, if you not only paint together, but also construct together—again alternately, each person doing one level. See how much you can or want to adjust yourself according to your perception of the other person's intention. Absolute silence is the climax of this exercise.

If you talk or even argue, you are certainly only in the left half of your brain—how then can you sense where your partner is?

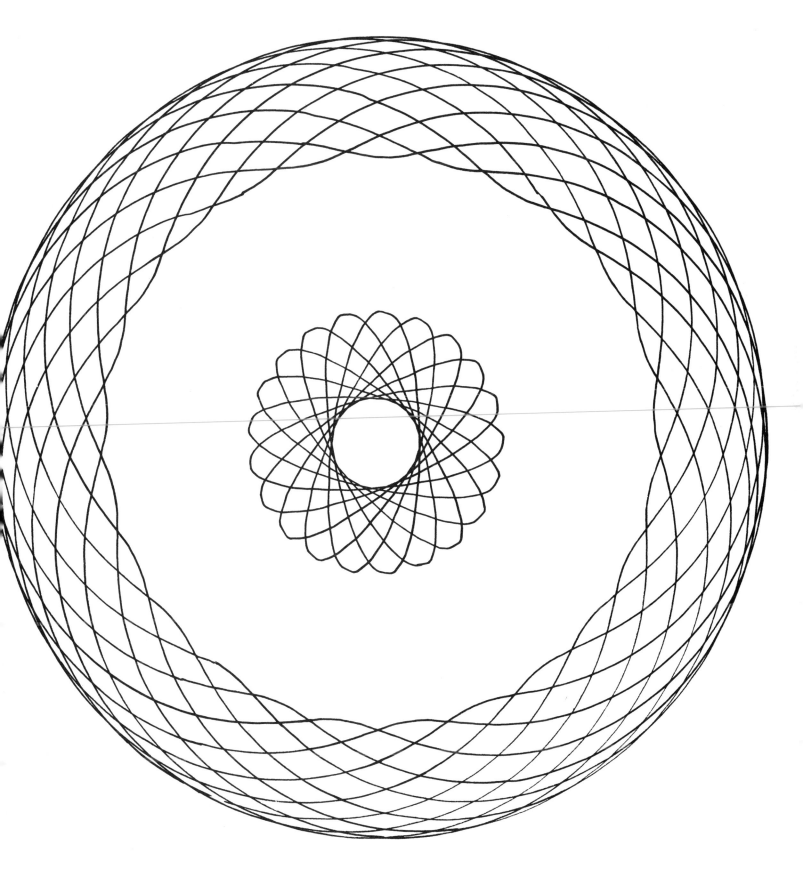

Of course you can expand the Mandala to the whole group. For example, you can draw a large Mandala on a large paper (e.g., wrapping paper), you can sit or lie around it and then paint alternately, layer by layer, or all at once in the direction of the common center—with watercolors or even finger paint. You can have a structure or only the center-point; you can be silent or talk. You can determine rules beforehand or simply begin. Yes, you can even lay a member of the group in the middle and paint the Mandala onto his/her skin—making the person part of the Mandala. There are simply no limits to your fantasy . . . besides the ones that you impose on it yourself. The whole thing can become a funny party-happening or an optical prayer like the rose windows of the Gothic . . . and it is all the same.

WARNING

Do not take any of these games seriously.
Games are not meant to be taken seriously,
otherwise they would not be games, after all.
And think once in a while about the cosmic
game . . .

When at some point somebody is insulted on this
journey through the world of the Mandalas, he/
she has made a "mistake" somewhere, and therefore gets a new chance:
He/she may proceed to the beginning of the book.
In the Mandala there are an unlimited number of
chances.

Snowflakes

Snowflakes

277

There are no two snowflakes that are the same. They are all slightly different and have their own character. But nevertheless they all came out of the same idea, that the snow crystals are equal to the other Mandalas—and to human beings.

Snowflakes

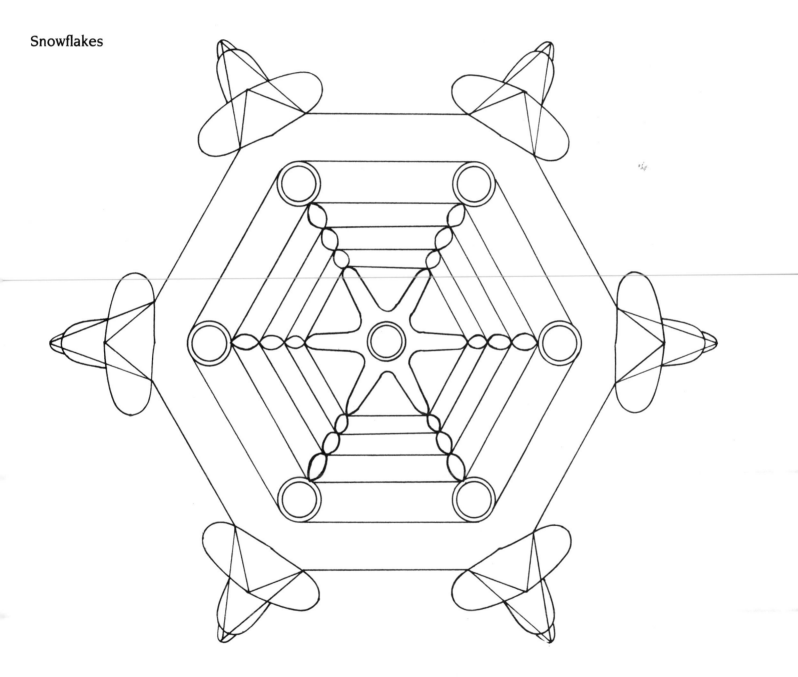

Snowflakes

With this snowstorm I want to say good-bye to you—knowing that we can meet again in each Mandala.

Snowflakes

Snowflakes

GLOSSARY

Aaron: elder brother of Moses; first high priest of the Jews

Aesculapius: Greek god of medicine and healing

Akasha: the unmanifested; spirit

alchemy: a medieval chemical science and speculative philosophy whose aim is to transmute base metals into gold, to discover a universal cure for disease, and to discover a means of indefinitely prolonging life

Allah: the name of the deity in Islam

American Indian: Native Americans, so called here to distinguish them from residents or natives of India

antipode: a direct or diametrical opposite, such as the black point in the white field of the T'ai Chi symbol

Aphrodite: Greek goddess of love, affection, and social interaction

Aquinas, St. Thomas: 13th-century Italian philosopher and theologian

archetype: an original model on which other, similar things are patterned

Asana: (Yoga) body positions patterned after animals or plants, used for exercise or meditation

Athanor: an occult hill whose winds, mists, wells, basins, fire, and rain all have alchemistic symbolism

aura: (esoteric) a usually invisible energy field surrounding an entity, living and nonliving; the field encompasses the entity, nurturing it to grow, mature, die. The aura displays many colors depending on the individual's health, state of mind, etc., and is visible to human beings who have developed the capability of seeing it.

aureole: radiant light projecting out from an individual's body or head, perceived physically or clairvoyantly, often represented in images of sacred personages.

birthplace of love (mussels): Oysters are traditionally considered an aphrodisiac.

Brahma: God in his creator aspect as one of the Hindu trinity

Brahman: a Hindu of the highest caste, traditionally assigned to the priesthood

Buddhism: one of the great religions of the world; the predominant Eastern philosophy

caduceus: the symbolic staff of a herald; a representation of a staff with two snakes entwined around it, topped by a pair of wings and a globe. The entwining represents the Kundalini power (*see below*) crossing at the Chakra points of the body. Associated with Hermes; used as a symbol for the practice of medicine

cardinal point: one of the four principal compass points: north, east, south, west

Cathar: a member of one of various ascetic Christian sects flourishing in the later Middle Ages, teaching that matter is evil, and professing faith in an angelic Christ who did not really undergo human birth or death

Chakra: a vortex of concentrated etheric energy, sometimes known as a psychic center; there are seven major Chakras in the human body, from the base of the spine to the crown of the head.

chasuble: sleeveless outer vestment worn by the officiating priest at Mass

circle: symbol representing infinity and eternity, having no beginning and no end (e.g., a ring)

clockwise or counterclockwise: The sun's course is clockwise (esoteric: deosil), circling to the right, which is considered to be the "normal," proper, and constructive order of circular movements. Counterclockwise (esoteric: widdershins) movements are used in working with negative, evil, or destructive forces, since these movements are believed to repudiate universal rule.

cosmos: an orderly, harmonious, systematic universe, functioning with purpose and meaning

cult: a system of persons who are bound together by the same ideal, principle, or leader, usually of a religious nature; a system or sect that becomes the object of devotion.

dervish: a Sufi holy man and psychic, noted for devotional exercises such as bodily movements leading to a trance, especially whirling and chanting. The movements are said to work in harmony with a polarity "energy" that keeps the dancers from becoming tired or dizzy.

Dhikr: (Sufi) a dance or method of worship to produce a state of ritual ecstasy in order to accelerate the contact of one's mind with the world mind, or to put oneself into a pre-trance state

Druid: (ancient Britain) one of an ancient Celtic priesthood appearing in Irish and Welsh sagas and Christian legends; maintained by some to be Buddhists who came to Britain during the Iron Age; learned class of Celtic people of Gaul, including philosophers, magistrates, priests, psychics, astrologers, mediums

Ego: here, the working consciousness of I, me, the separateness from others (*see* Self)

emptiness: (metaphysical) state of consciousness during meditation when one is unaware of time, space, or movement, but instead feels a void, or "pure being"

entity: that portion of a (usually) deceased human or animal that has not yet completely blended into spirit; a negative or positive "energy" field that makes its presence known, often in a geographical area or in emotional circumstances that relate to former earth life or lives

esoteric: refers to information and knowledge that is understood by the specially initiated alone; also that better understood by the "feeling" nature than by the intellect

Essene: member of a learned monastic brotherhood of Jews in Palestine from the second century B.C. to the second century A.D., including both men and women. They were teachers and record keepers. It is believed that Jesus Christ was taught by the Essenes; some of his stated principles followed those of the Essenes.

evil eye: a powerful glare from the eyes that catches and holds another's attention. If used with evil intent, the recipient of the glare may be temporarily hypnotized and his/her subconscious opened to hypnotic suggestion; or unpleasant events may occur in the recipient's life.

ex orient lux: (Latin) from the East, light

Gandhi, Mohandas K., honorific Mahatma: (1869–1948) a Hindu religious and political leader; led opposition to British rule in India via nonviolent disobedience, hunger strikes, and boycotts. Helped negotiate Indian independence after World War II; assassinated by a Hindu secret organization that blamed him for the partition of India into separate Hindu and Muslim states.

Gothic: as used here, pertinent to an architectural style of Western Europe from the 12th through the 15th century. One of its features is a pointed arch, especially with a joint rather than a keystone at its apex.

Guna(s): the vital life force, encompassing a primordial quality of motion and harmonious working with primordial intelligence

guru: a personal religious teacher or spiritual guide who, by pointing out the right way to live, inspires the disciple to follow the disciple's intended path, especially in Hinduism

Hermes: messenger and herald of the Greek gods; he escorted the souls of the dead to Hades. He was represented as wearing winged sandals and bearing the caduceus, his staff of office.

Hermes Trismegistus (Thoth): "Thrice Greatest Hermes"—Greek name for Thoth, Egyptian god of wisdom, learning, and literature. As scribe of the gods he was credited with authorship of 42 sacred books that the Greeks thus called "Hermetic." Hermetic also applied to mystic literature of post–Early Christian times.

I Ching: (China, approximately second millennium B.C.) "Book of Change"—a guide to comprehensive self-realization, often used for divination. Several layers of text have been given numerous levels of interpretation. Sayings are attached to sixty-four signs and each of the six lines of which every sign is constructed. Objects (yarrow sticks, coins, etc.) are tossed to construct the hexagram(s). The esoteric notation of the hexagrams describes elements, processes, and experiences in developing the body and mind.

Indians: here, natives or residents of India

iridology: study of the eyes to diagnose their related body parts

Isis: chief female deity of Egyptian mythology; wife of Osiris and mother of Horus. The cult of Isis was widespread through Greece and Rome.

Islam: the religious faith of Muslims, including belief in Allah as the sole deity and Muhammad as his Prophet

Kabbalah: Jewish doctrine or system of theosophy. The Tree of Life symbolizes the spiritual unfoldment of the individual.

Kali: (Hindu) a female etheric world intelligence in charge of destruction

Karma: the force generated by one's actions in previous lives. Its consequences (partially) determine one's destiny.

Kether: represents the number 1; the first manifestation; light

Knights Templar: (medieval) members of the military religious Order of the Poor Knights of Christ, called the Knights of the Temple of Solomon from their house in Jerusalem. Formed during the Crusades to protect pilgrims and Christianity, the Knights Templar rapidly became one of Europe's most powerful organizations. They were important in the internal struggles among the Crusaders as well as in the fight against the infidel, and took part in all the important sieges and battles. Persecution of the wealthy Templars organization by Philip IV of France brought disgrace and a mysterious end to the organization.

Koan: (Zen Buddhism) an unanswerable paradox designed to stop useless inner babble and force the mind to gain sudden intuitive enlightenment

kraal: a village of southern African natives; an enclosure for animals, especially in southern Africa

Kundalini: a concentrated field of intelligent, cosmic, invisible "energy" that begins in the base of the spine and rises through the Chakras to the crown as the individual evolves through incarnations. By nature Kundalini is feminine polarity.

lemniscate: a lying-down figure eight that, in both mathematics and esoterics, represents infinity

Lingam: (Hindu) a stylized phallic symbol for masculine positive cosmic polarity. The stylized female (negative) symbol is Yoni.

Logos: the divine wisdom manifest in the creation, government, and redemption of the world, and often identified with the second person of the trinity

Lotus, thousand-petalled: a many-petalled white water lily whose bloom is nearly one foot across; "the crown of glory"; sacred symbol (e.g., the emanations of divine radiance from the crown Chakra that indicate the highest spiritual development)

Lucifer: "light-giver"; first erroneously though now traditionally equated with the fallen angel Satan. "Lucifer" connotes star, and originally referred to the morning or evening star.

Magician: The first card of the major arcana in a Tarot card deck, signifying (e.g.) the right use of will. In Zoroastrianism (600 B.C.) a magician was an educated scientist and alchemist who sought to understand the purpose of mankind on earth, utilized the power of thought and sound, and performed psychic healings.

Mandala: (MUN-duh-luh) (Sanskrit) "the mystic circle"; simultaneously representative of sound, light, color, form, rhythm, and harmony

Manichaeans: members of a third-century Persian sect who believed in release of the spirit from matter through asceticism

manifest: (adj.) clearly apparent; visible; touchable; (verb) to bring to or present in physical form

mantra: a sound used as a focal point in meditation

Mantram: a symbol of supreme reality; a holy name or spiritual formula used to focus the mental processes

Maya: illusion. The world that we know is "illusion"; the spiritual world is "reality."

Mayans or Mayas: members of a group of Indian peoples of southern Mexico and Central America, 250–900 A.D.

Meridians: (China) Twelve invisible, electrical nerve "fluid" lines that run from the tips of the toes and fingers to the head area. The meridians are thought to connect all the major organs and glands as well as the human body to the movements of sun, moon, earth, and planets.

metaphysics: a doctrine that each is a part of all else, that we are interdependent, and that each contributes to the whole

Minotaur: (mythology) The monster son of Pasiphaë (wife of Minos, king of Crete), whose passion for a sacrificial bull resulted in the birth of a creature with a human male body and a bull's head. The Minotaur was imprisoned in a labyrinth constructed by Daedalus. After Minos's victory in war over Athens, he demanded a regular sacrifice of young men and women to the Minotaur. Theseus, as one of his heroic feats, slew the Minotaur.

Muldhara: the root Chakra; a vortex of etheric energy at the base of the spine

Muslim: an adherent of the faith of Islam

Nadis: The "nervous system" of the astral body, connecting the astral brain with the physical brain. One's mind can strengthen this system and direct it for use in psychic skills including healing.

nimbus: emanations of light seen around the heads of great spiritual beings and religious figures; various colors; in form a circle, triangle, or square. Also seen as backlighting when the sun is behind any observed object.

Nirvana: bliss, spiritual enlightenment or illumination that releases the individual from suffering, birth, and death; diminishment of personality and identification with the higher self

Orient: the East; also lustre or radiance, as of a pearl; (verb) to cause the chief portion (of a building) to be in, or point towards, the east; to arrange in a specific position, especially in regard to the compass points

pagoda: a Far Eastern tower of several stories, each story with a roof curving upward; erected as a temple or memorial

Paradise: the Garden of Eden; a place or condition of joy

Parsifal: a figure in Arthurian legend whose search for the Holy Grail ends at the castle of Amfortas, the Fisher King, where the hero heals the wounded king and thus the king's people

placebo: an inactive, nonmedicinal substance given to placate a patient, or used as a control in an experiment

polar: diametrically opposite or even conflicting: man/woman, rough/smooth

potential: existing in possibility; already existing on another level; capable of being brought into being

prayer carpet: a small rug used by Muslims to kneel on while praying. Animations of "flying carpets" derive their humor and delight from the otherworldly experience or state that one can achieve through prayer or meditation.

Prophet, the: Muhammad, the founder of Islam (570–632 A.D.)

pyramid, step-pyramid: a construction of four triangles placed together that, when correctly dimensioned, yields condensed "energy" inside it, especially the top one-third. A step-pyramid, with steps leading to the top, represents ascent to higher consciousness.

Pythagoras: (580–500 B.C.) Greek philosopher and mathematician; founded a religious brotherhood, one of whose beliefs was that the essence of all things was number, and that all things could be expressed numerically. Pythagoras worked out a system of numerology based on 1 through 9.

rainbow colors, six: the seven spectrum colors of the rainbow: violet, indigo, blue, green, yellow, orange, and red. Some schools of thought leave out indigo, a dark grey-blue.

rishi: a psychic; one who can intensify concentration on a focal point, or enter an altered state of consciousness at will

sacral: here, pertaining to the sacred

Self: the subconscious, the spiritual basis of one's being (*see* Ego).

Shiva: a male deity of the Vedas. He represents divine creative power, time, death; positive polarity; in the Hindu trinity, god of destruction and regeneration

Sisyphus: son of Aeolus in Greek myth; a trickster-hero. After death, in order to keep him from tricking his way out of Hades a second time, he was sentenced to roll his stone eternally uphill.

square: first of the Tattwa symbols; representation of earth/earthiness

stupa: a dome-shaped mount or tower serving as a Buddhist shrine

Sufi: a Muslim mystic

Sushumna: an ethereal and physical tiny holly "nerve" acting as a tube in the spinal column. Filled with vital "life force," it runs from the base of the spine to the crown Chakra, where it connects with the "silver cord" that makes a human being part of the universe.

Swastika: a cross with four bent arms all turning the same way; religious symbol; fertility symbol. Tilted left, it was the Nazi party symbol of destruction.

T'ai Chi: (China, 1000 B.C.) "the whole circle"; "The Absolute" in Chinese cosmology; (T'ai Chi Ch'uan) slow, nonstrenuous exercises in specific patterns for conditioning the entire organism

Tantra: a discipline the goal of which is to set free the spark of divine light in every human being

Tao, Taoism: (China, Vedic) "The Way"; the seamless web of unbroken movement and change filled with undulations, which does not itself change. The Tao is the "uncarved block" devoid of any definable shape, the matrix of time, being, not-being, the Great Whole of continuous duration, infinite space, and infinite change.

Tarot: a set of cards for the purpose of divination. There are 22 major arcana and 56 suit cards (rods, cups, swords, coins), each with multiple symbols and all related to numerology, astrology, and the Kabbalah. The querent asks questions. The reader shuffles the cards and lays them in one of numerous spreads. From the symbols on the cards and their positions in relation to one another, the answer may be derived.

Tattwas: plain geometric figures used to stimulate the mental, nervous, and intuitive faculties to receive information

third eye: a psychic area located between and just above the eyebrows; inside, it "opens" to the pineal, the pituitary, and the thalamus glands. The glands act together to process cosmic information into a form one can recognize and use.

thousand-petalled lotus: *see* Lotus

transsubstantiation: the doctrine that the bread and wine of the Eucharist are transformed into the true presence of Christ, even though their appearance remains unchanged

ultramundane: beyond or not of this world

Vedas: scriptures that form the basis of the Hindu religion; received by the rishis as a directly heard literature of chants and recitations

Venus: a Roman goddess of love, beauty, and charm

Vishnu: the preserver god of the Hindu sacred triad; an exalted god or angel who elects to be incarnated on earth during a particular period to help the righteous and to give guidance

Yantra: (Hindu) a symbolic diagram, used as a focus for meditation

Yin/Yang: a circle divided into two equal parts by a double-curved line. The dark half is Yin (feminine, negative) energy; the light half is Yang (masculine, positive) energy. Symbol shows the polarity within the wholeness.

Yoni: *see* Lingam

Zen: (China, Japan) a branch of Buddhism, though not a religion; a highly intellectual metaphysical philosophy that concentrates on meditation to reach the silence

GLOSSARY REFERENCES

The American Heritage Dictionary of the English Language. New York: Dell, 1970.

Bletzer, June. *The Donning International Encyclopedic Psychic Dictionary.* Virginia Beach: Donning, 1986.

The Columbia Encyclopedia. New York: Columbia University Press, 1950.

Davidson, Gustav. *A Dictionary of Angels.* New York: Macmillan, 1967.

Evans, Bergen. *Dictionary of Mythology.* New York: Dell, 1970.

Hamilton, Edith. *Mythology.* New York: New American Library, 1969.

Robinson, Herbert Spencer. *The Dictionary of Biography.* Lanham: Littlefield, 1975.

Spence, Lewis. *An Encylopaedia of Occultism.* New York: Citadel Press, 1960.

Webster's Ninth New Collegiate Dictionary. Springfield: Merriam-Webster, 1988.

INDEX